HOT RODS

HOT RODS

ROB LEICESTER WAGNER

PHOTOGRAPHS BY RANDY LORENTZEN

MetroBooks

MetroBooks

An Imprint of Friedman/Fairfax Publishers

Library of Congress Cataloging-in-Publication Data

Wagner, Rob
    Hot rods / Rob Leicester Wagner.
        p.   cm.
    Includes bibliographical references and index.
    ISBN 1-56799-822-4
    1. Hot rods.   I. Title.
TL236.3.W34 1999
629.228'6--dc21   99-31540
                            CIP

Editor: Ann Kirby
Art Director: Kevin Ullrich
Designer: John Gaines
Photography Editor: Wendy Missan
Production Manager: Richela Fabian

Color separations by Spectrum Pte Ltd.
Printed in Hong Kong by Sing Cheong Printing Company Ltd.

3 5 7 9 10 8 6 4 2

For bulk purchases and special sales, please contact:
Friedman/Fairfax Publishers
Attention: Sales Department
15 West 26th Street
New York, NY 10010
212/685-6610 FAX 212/685-1307

Visit our website:
http://www.metrobooks.com

Photography ©Randy Loventzen
(except p. 63 top and bottom ©Walt Weiss)

For Deniece

ACKNOWLEDGMENTS

Special thanks to the following California hot rod and musclecar enthusiasts for their help in writing this book: Chet Harris of Riverside ('65 Plymouth Barracuda), Wayne and Margie Jenkins of Cathedral City ('48 Ford Anglia), Richard Cortez of Rialto ('39 Pontiac), and Gary and Judy Stevens of Riverside ('41 Chevrolet coupe).

FOLLOWING PAGES: *The Plymouth Prowler was an early effort by Chrysler, now DaimlerChrysler, to tap into the baby boomer set's renewed interest in hot rodding. It has become an instant collectible.*

THE HOT ROD
GOES LEGIT

At several Southern California car shows throughout the year, there is—tucked in a corner somewhere—a very special, attention-getting 1967 Plymouth Barracuda painted black and white and adorned with the black and white Los Angeles County sheriff's logo on the door and lightbar on the roof. Not your average patrol car, it bears little resemblance to the vehicles routinely used by sheriffs deputies.

A member of Team Sheriff Racing, the Barracuda is part of a marketing effort by the Los Angeles County Sheriff's Department's Youth Foundation program to keep young people off of drugs and out of gangs. This "cop car" is powered by a 450-cubic-inch B-1 V-8 engine that offers 700 horsepower. Power is transferred through a B&M transmission. Its sister car is a 1987 Buick Grand National, driven by Deputy Bill Chaffin. Under the hood is a 274-cubic-inch V-6 that generates a nonturbo 580 horsepower, complete with a Hogan's manifold and B&M transmission. Both cars stand at the ready to hit the drag strip.

A TALE OF OUTLAWS AND CELEBRITIES

A generation ago, cops—and, yes, even the Los Angeles County Sheriff's Department—were knuckling down on hot rodders. Your custom rod riding too low? A fix-it ticket. Headlamps not aligned properly? The same, kiddo. Tread on those fat tires not deep enough? It's off the street.

Today the hot rod enjoys new respectability. Hot rodding is an acceptable hobby and a multibillion-dollar industry. Basketball star Shaquille O'Neal, Van Halen bassist Michael Anthony, and even ex-supermodel Cheryl Tiegs have strutted their stuff in customized hot rods. Police departments throughout the country are finding sponsors and a willing officer to customize a car and wow hot rod wannabes with outrageous styling and a fast time on the track.

Such names as Ed "Big Daddy" Roth, Boyd Coddington, and George and Sam Barris hold legendary status as the pioneers of the hot rod and custom rod. But hot rodding no longer consists of a bunch of guys getting together at the local body shop to map out a cruise night. Now it's groups like the Anaheim, California–based Cruise Productions that organize hot rod shows and cruises for such big corporate names as Del Taco and Pep Boys.

PAGE 8: *Cruise nights mean '34 Fords, Mercurys, muscle-cars, and customized pickups congregating in the parking lot of the gaudiest '50s diner in town.*

PAGE 9: *From the air cleaner to the manifolds, filler cap, and water pump, the chrome is clean enough to eat off of in top quality hot rods.*

OPPOSITE: *The 1940 Ford sedan is a favorite among hot rod enthusiasts for customizing. Its clean industrial design and modest body trim give it a clean look. The front end was lowered slightly with only flames and moon hubcaps giving it a slightly modified look. Note the nod to yesteryear with the wide whitewall tires.*

And, finally, to put something of a stamp of approval on the 1990s version of hot rodding, Detroit automakers such as the Chrysler Corporation have gotten into the game, introducing instant collectibles such as the Plymouth Prowler and Dodge Viper.

Like rock 'n' roll music, hot rod and custom rod collecting and cruising have gone respectable—no longer an outlaw art form but part of mainstream pop culture. Gone are James Dean in his Mercury, and Jan and Dean worrying about "Dead Man's Curve." Today's hot rodders are sipping sodas in lawn chairs next to their '66 Chevelle or customized '53 Studebaker Starlight coupe, and rocking the baby stroller at car shows. Burn a little rubber in the parking lot? You're 86'd, pal.

THE LONG ROAD TO RESPECTABILITY

It wasn't always that way, and perhaps that's for the best. Hot and custom rodding first gained notoriety in postwar California, but there were hints of it as far back as the early 1930s, when teenagers and young men prowled wrecking yards to cannibalize Model Ts and Model As to build their own cars. They left off the fenders to give them some personality and a decidedly blue-collar look, and tweaked the engines a bit to make them faster, louder, and more powerful.

As early as 1941, commercial custom jobs began to appear. George and Sam Barris tackled a 1936 Plymouth at their Roseville, California, shop by fitting it with a Nash grille,

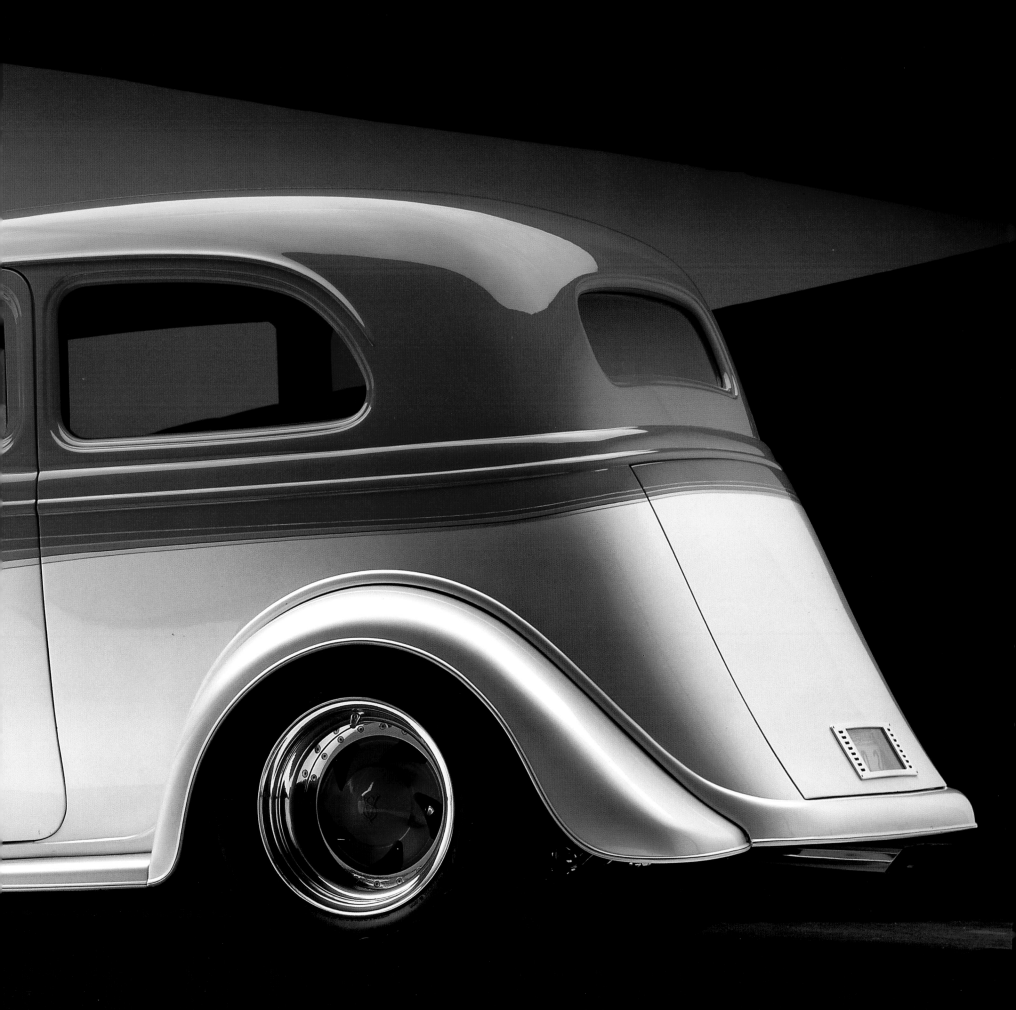

1940 Oldsmobile bumpers, teardrop skirts, and baldy hubcaps. It was topped with a powder-blue paint job.

The term hot rod has come to mean different things to different people. Essentially, however, it is a car that is modified beyond factory specs. A set of wide tires and mag wheels may make a '66 Chevy Nova a hot rod to one fella but just a stock car with big tires to another. For the purposes of this book any car that has been tinkered with under the hood to enhance performance or had work done to the body to give it panache and style beyond what the original factory designers intended is a hot rod. The exceptions are musclecars and factory lightweights. These cars are built by the factory but because of their massive power they earn a membership in the ever-evolving hot rod club.

Consider the many hot rod genres that have emerged from the original rods of the highboy, shoebox Ford, or that icon of all hot rods, the '49 Merc. There is the tried and true hot rod

PAGES 12–13: *This 1934 Ford Crown Victoria or "Vicky" two-door sedan sports a three-tone paint scheme.*

OPPOSITE: *Another '40 Ford, this one a DeLuxe coupe. Owners appreciate the timeless quality of the prewar design. This model is even more modest than most, appearing virtually stock right down to the bumpers.*

ABOVE: *A customized air intake on a souped-up Corvette.*

LEFT: *Moon hubcaps, wide whites, and a touch of flame give this car the classic touch.*

that puts an emphasis on performance rather than on cruising. It's a car that puts its reputation on straight-line or drag racing. The street rod is a throwback to another era, when fenderless Fords and Model Ts earned a reputation by racing at dry lake beds and circle tracks. Today street rods are more show than performance, but they are certainly capable of hitting speeds in the three digits if put to the test.

The custom rod is all show and maybe a little go, with attention paid primarily to the body and interior. Chopped tops, shaved door handles, and several layers of lacquer give custom rods a distinct look. The lowrider, although inexplicably shunned by many hot rod enthusiasts, also falls in a category of hot rods, with its low-slung look, wild paint jobs, intricate murals on the panels, and flashy, chrome-laden engines.

Factory musclecars with engines tweaked (but often left completely stock) fall into another category. The late '60s and early '70s heyday of big factory-built engines generating a lot of horsepower has earned Chevelles, 'Cudas, Chargers, and Mustangs a spot in the hot rod lineup. Another brand of factory car, the factory lightweight, is considerably different from the musclecars. Built in limited quantities to qualify as production cars, these factory lightweights—stripped down to the bare essentials to enhance speed—were raced on drag strips to earn top trophies and accolades from the automotive press in an effort to boost sales of models to the general public.

The last of the genre is the pickup truck, which in the past decade has emerged as the '90s version of the Mercury, Olds Rocket, and flathead V-8 Fords. Often chopped and lowered,

This 1967 Chevelle pro street rod is classic musclecar chic and a favorite among racers. But these babies never saw the light of day in GM-sponsored drag racing against Fords because the automaker pulled the plug on such racing. But by the early '70s, Chevelles were back on the track with 460-horsepower engines.

the pickup has gained considerable attention at car shows as a relatively inexpensive alternative to other custom and street rods.

POSTWAR RISE OF THE HOT ROD

Two distinctive groups put hot rodding on the map: returning World War II veterans and disenfranchised Mexican-Americans from East Los Angeles. Legitimizing the hobby was *Hot Rod* magazine, which debuted in January 1948 and is still published today.

California in the late 1940s was a fertile field for hot rodding. At a time when people rarely drove more than 500 miles (800km) from home, those with a desire to open up their engines craved the kind of unsnarled roadways and huge, flat vacant lots that defined the postwar landscape in California. Southern California, and Los Angeles in particular, gave license

BELOW: *Custom rods can go to extremes, like this 1929 Ford Model A, which has been transformed into a crew cab with bed.*

to freewheeling driving, whether on dry lake beds like Rosamond or Muroc north of Los Angeles or the empty fields in Orange County where John Wayne Airport now stands. Further, celebrities like Zeppo Marx (who raced a turbocharged Mercedes-Benz, notably in one famed race match against a Duesenberg SJ at Muroc Dry Lake) had already sown the seeds of hot rodding in California during the 1930s.

When the war was over, auto racing took off both in Europe and in the States. Many young men of the time lived and died by the hot rod. In the California of the late '40s and early '50s, more than a few young men who had survived the German onslaught in the world war or, later, on the battlefields of Korea would die at Muroc, Rosamond, and the Bonneville Salt Flats in crude hot rods. Safety was rarely a consideration.

These early daredevils began to form clubs like the Knight Riders, the Outlaws, and the Bungholers. In East Los Angeles, hot rodders and customizers began cruising along Whittier Boulevard and Brooklyn Avenue. For Latinos in the Los Angeles area, the trend toward hot rodding was rooted in more than mere thrill-seeking. The 1942 Sleepy Lagoon murder case—in which nine Mexican-American men went to prison for a crime they did not commit—and the 1943 Zoot Suit riots left an indelible mark on the community. Denied basic recreational services, Latinos began a number of local car clubs.

Run-ins with the Los Angeles Police Department and Los Angeles County Sheriff's Department were commonplace. The newspapers, especially Hearst newspapers like the *Los Angeles Examiner* and the *Los Angeles Herald-Express,* were unforgiving in their coverage of this new and perceived reckless hobby, no matter who was behind the wheel. A campaign to rid the streets of this alleged menace was launched and the term "hot rodder" was born. It was meant as a derogatory term, but hot rodders adopted the moniker as their own as an act of defiance. In short order, it was an accepted label for any young person driving or showing a car that was customized either in body or under the hood.

George and Sam Barris typified the postwar California car culture in terms of customizing. Born in Chicago, the boys moved to Roseville, California, with their parents in 1928. As

they grew older they began tinkering with cars with some light customizing. They flirted with hot rod racing at local dry lakes and drag strips, but found that customizing, not racing or building bigger engines under the hood, was their forte.

By the time World War II ended, the boys were experienced customizers. They opened a new customizing shop at 7674 Compton Avenue in Los Angeles, and it became a popular hangout for hot rodders. Sunday trips to the Corona Speedway to show and race cars were the highlight of the weekend for the Barrises and their friends. Their first major custom job was a 1941 Buick convertible, and it proved to be a breakthrough car for the brothers. It featured a 1941 Cadillac grille, Oldsmobile bumpers, fade-away fenders, frenched headlamps, custom taillamps, and the never-before-seen Royal Metallic Maroon paint job. It stood a mere 4 feet, 10 inches (1.5m) tall after the Barrises channeled the frame and shortened the convertible top by 4 inches (10cm). The fenders were hand-formed and blended into the body without seams. Under the hood was

BELOW: *An outrageous, high-performance street rod, the '40 Willys Gasser has many fans among the hot rod set.*

a chromed full-race Buick 225-cubic-inch engine. The car was featured on the May 1948 cover of the fledgling *Road and Track* magazine. The media attention gave Barris's Custom Shop a boost in business.

IN PRINT AND ON FILM: THE FAD THAT WOULDN'T DIE

What could simply have been a 1940s fad, like zoot suits, jitterbugging, and the Andrews Sisters, turned into a cultural icon that transcends generations. *Road and Track and Motor Trend* magazines solidified the hobby and gave it a much-needed lift during those early battles with law enforcement and the mainstream media. And therein lies the early success of the hot rod hobby: the power of the media.

Where the mainstream Los Angeles press saw hot rods and custom rods as a threat to the community, enthusiasts appreciated the artistry and technology of the modified automobile. Magazines like *Motor Trend*, *Road and Track*, and *Hot Rod* (and, later on, in the 1970s, *Lowrider*) spread the word that hot rodding could be a wholesome hobby. To cement its place in history and ensure that it deserved a long life, the hobby was secured with the debut of *Hot Rod* magazine in

January 1948. Founded by Robert "Pete" Petersen, the magazine was "published to inform and entertain those interested in automobiles whose bodies and engines have been rebuilt in the quest for better performances and appearances." Touted as giving its readers the "World's Most Complete Hot Rod Coverage," Hot Rod's first cover featured Eddie Hulse of Compton, California, driving Regg Schlemmer's Class C roadster at the El Mirage Dry Lake on October 19, 1947; at El Mirage Hulse averaged 136.05 mph (218.9kph). The magazine also featured technical advice, results, and standings from tracks and dry lakes, and the usual assortment of cheesecake art featuring girls with car parts.

Hot Rod initially put its attention on racing at dry lakes and tracks but soon expanded to street and custom rods, where looks were equally important as performance. The founding of the magazine coincided with the first hot rod exposition sponsored by the Southern California Timing Association. The exhibit was organized to show off the best designed and engineered cars belonging to some of the Association's seven hundred members. The show was staged in an effort not only to draw publicity for the Association but to put a serious face on the safety issue by dispelling the notion that hot rodding was a hobby enjoyed by reckless youth. To drive the point home, the Association invited the Los Angeles Police Department to conduct a driver's education seminar.

Television and movies further legitimized the hot rod as a fashion statement, and perhaps forever changed the image of hot rodders from outlaw bandits to clean-cut kids in search of fun. The early-1950s sitcom *The Life of Riley*, starring William Bendix, featured a '34 coupe with a '32 grille shell, with wide whitewall tires, moon hubcaps, and a chrome-plated V-8 with triple carbs, created by George Barris. Robert Young's wholesome 1961 television show *Window on Main Street* once featured another Barris hot rod, this one a 1927 T body with Buick Skylark wire wheels and a Dodge Red Ram Hemi engine. The hot rod got probably the most important sanction from the establishment in 1955, however, when the popular program Dragnet featured a '32 highboy.

Even such films as The Bachelor and the Bobby-Soxer (1947), with Cary Grant and Shirley Temple, and I Want You (1951), with Dana Andrews and Farley Granger, featured fenderless hot rods. These movies, mainstream middle-America fare, provided something of a boost for the burgeoning industry. Meanwhile, teenagers across the country got their first taste of hot rod excitement with teen rebel films like Rebel Without A Cause (1955), with James Dean and Natalie Wood, and High School Confidential! (1958), with Russ Tamblyn and Jan Sterling. By the 1960s popular music chimed in with its emphasis on cruising and beach-going. T-Birds, Woodies, and GTOs were expounded by the likes of The Beach Boys and Jan and Dean as an integral part of teen culture.

Print, film, and television had conspired against the conservative element to keep hot and custom rods on the streets by generating an image that defied the ugly portrait produced by the Hearst newspapers and accentuated the positive concepts. These young hot rodders were not hooligans defiling daughters and running wild in the streets. No, these were boys (and even some girls) next door who frequented sock hops, drive-ins, town boulevards, and sanctioned speedways. Soon the hot rod was a source for father-son bonding and dating rituals among teens.

OPPOSITE: *A '32 Ford highboy keeps its hood, with the only dash of color coming from the dramatic red grille and unseen red wheel rims.*

THE '60s BRING A NEW KIND OF HOT ROD

Custom deuce coupes gave way to bizarre creations by Big Daddy Roth and George Barris. High-octane funny cars debuted in the mid-'60s. The first factory musclecar debuted when Pontiac dropped a Tri-Power 389 V-8 into its intermediate Tempest and made it a GTO. The Chevelle SS, Shelby Mustang, Olds 4-4-2, Camaro Z/28, Plymouth Road Runner, Dodge Charger, and Dodge Challenger with varying degrees of muscle were all part of the new hot rod scene. Here were cars powered by sizable engines like the Chevy 396 and 454, the Boss 429 and 427, the Mopar Hemis, and 383s and 440s.

As far as musclecar enthusiasts were concerned, this kind of hot rodding could go on forever. It also might have spelled the end to the traditional '50s era of highboys and '51 Mercs if it hadn't been for the U.S. government. Safety and emission regulations and the oil crisis of 1973 put a cap on unbridled power. What emerged were compact cars and a dramatic climb in Japanese and European imports equipped with puny four-bangers and the occasional V-6 engine.

The spirit and popularity of the musclecar came to a climax with the ultimate road movie, *Vanishing Point* (1971), a cult classic that featured Barry Newman ripping from Denver to San Francisco in a Dodge Challenger in less than fifteen hours, all to the beat of a rock sound track. George Lucas followed it up a few years later—in the midst of the government clampdown—with a little film that was intended to be nothing more than a tribute to his youth. *American Graffiti* (1973) was a celebration of '50s-style cruising, anchored by the exploits of Paul LeMat's deuce coupe and Suzanne Somers's Thunderbird. This "coming of age" film struck a chord with moviegoers in the early 1970s, especially with baby boomers nostalgic about the carefree cruising of their youth. The film jump started the careers of young actors like Harrison Ford and Richard Dreyfuss, and brought the classic hot rod back into style.

Since the '70s hot rods have come to include myriad categories of the car culture, with lowriders, street or factory rods, and custom rods and trucks. They're all hot rods to a degree but appeal to specific enthusiasts.

OPPOSITE: *Custom chrome rims are a staple of hot rod styling.*

BELOW: *Only in the last decade have pickup trucks made a serious foray into the hot rod scene. Customizing trucks, however, has become increasingly popular, as evidenced by this lowered '68 Chevy.*

STILL CRUISING: MODERN HOT RODS

Musclecars never went away, of course. But where was the serious car nut in the '70s going to find a new car that could be customized into a genuine muscle machine? Good candidates were found in car showrooms. Gas-guzzling power was sapped from the musclecar of the late '60s and early '70s, but with a little tweaking a new kind of rod appeared. The mini musclecar was born in the mid-1970s with the Chevrolet Monza, Ford Maverick, Olds Starfire, and Pontiac Astre. The Buick Skyhawk also found its way into speed shops for massive transformations into lightweight hot rods. Enthusiasts also reached back for Chevy IIs, Volkswagens, and second-generation Camaros for their hot rides.

There are some fine examples of late '70s mini muscles today. Scott Dillingham of Indiana owns a '78 Ford Mustang fitted with a blown 2.8-liter V-6. These Mustangs inspired little confidence in buyers when first introduced. Their styling is less than dramatic and Detroit workmanship of the era was left wanting. But even the ugliest duckling has a chance to shine with the proper attention. Displacing 173 cubic inches, the engine is equipped with a supercharger and Holley 600 carb. Pistons are 8:1 models and complemented by Crane camshaft, pushrods, and valve springs. The blower delivers an 11-pound (5kg) boost to the engine. Hooker headers are also part of the ensemble. All this gives the little pony 320 horsepower and 200 pounds-feet of torque. State-of-the-art Ford chassis components make the Mustang tough, with a Ford 9-inch (23cm) rear end and Ford rack-and-pinion steering for exceptional handling.

The 1980s brought corporate sponsorships to drag strips. The aftermarket industry exploded, giving anyone and everyone with a fat enough wallet the opportunity to buy reproduction hot rods, crate engines, and enough accessories to make any car a rolling advertisement for the next Specialty Equipment Market Association (SEMA) convention. Detroit, meanwhile, perfected computer technology that allowed for lower smog emissions and better performance and efficiency.

If the '80s were about new technology and corporate sponsorship, the '90s might be identified as the retro decade, as folks looked to the past for new-old ideas. Lead-sleds and fat-fendered bodies found their way back. Four-door sedans and station wagons from the late '50s and early '60s (how about a '60 Rambler, boys, or a '61 Chevy Biscayne?) were suddenly prized. The Chrysler Corporation seized on this retro surge by introducing the Plymouth Prowler, an open, needle-nose roadster with motorcycle fenders. Chrysler then heightened the excitement by offering a limited quantity of Prowlers in order to create a huge demand.

The '90s also proved to be the decade wherein drivers got behind the wheel again, and drove their babies not just across county lines but across state lines in caravans that included the family. _Hot Rod_ magazine sponsored a cross-country tour in 1995. By 1998, the ten-day, 2,800-mile (4,480km) pilgrimage across the heartland, from Los Angeles to Mt. Clemons, Michigan, was drawing hundreds of hot rod owners and their families.

The image of the hot rodder has changed significantly since the hobby's inception in prewar America. The average hot rodder today is no longer a teenager scouring wrecking yards (and more than a few parking lots) for parts. Today he's a respectable, financially secure family man. A 1998 survey conducted by SEMA showed that the average hot rodder is a thirty-eight-year-old male with a household income of $62,136.

When musclecars took center stage in automotive circles in the late 1960s, enthusiasts—not to mention aftermarket

accessories companies—feared that the hot rod industry would peter out. In the early '70s they had hoped the trend would last another five or ten years. More than a quarter century later they are still making the same prediction. Yes, the hot rodder has aged some since those halcyon days of preemission regulations and optional seat belts, but it seems that new blood routinely infused will keep it alive.

STREET *RODS*

Street rodding began as nothing more than illegal drags on local boulevards. Slowly, it migrated to oval dirt tracks, where police interference was less likely, but dirt, rocks, and debris wreaked havoc on bodies and undercarriages. By the late '30s, street rodders discovered Southern California's dry lake beds. This is where street rods earned their reputation for tough, high-speed driving over quarter-mile or mile distances. On any given Sunday, as many as half a dozen street rods raced abreast at Muroc or Bonneville. As the crowds and the fields of hot rods racing across the concrete-hard floor grew, this type of racing became as dangerous as the initial illegal street drags.

The Southern California Timing Association (SCTA) was formed to give these races some legitimacy, but dry lake racing came to a dead stop with the outbreak of World War II. The Air Force took over the dry lakes and racing moved back to the streets and quarter-mile oval tracks.

OPPOSITE: This '34 Ford three-window coupe is stripped of all chrome molding and its door handles are shaved. Custom shops now offer all-new remanufactured bodies and pans. A fully loaded '34 Ford three-window coupe can be constructed from scratch without a single original Ford factory part. DETAIL: The icon of a street rod. Huge intake systems provide plenty of air for hungry engines.

MR. FORD'S LITTLE DEUCE COUPE: THE CLASSIC STREET ROD

Deuce coupes and highboys are considered, as they have been for more than fifty years, the archetypal street rod. Often shorn of fenders and hoods and sporting a beefed-up V-8, they can knock the socks off of any factory stock car. Just about any car can be transformed into a street, but the '32 Ford coupe remains today perhaps the body of choice for true street rodders. Coming in a close second are late-'20s Fords and Chevrolets, and Fords and Pontiacs from the '30s.

The '32 Ford coupe, in the thick of virtually every illegal and sanctioned road race in Southern California, gained

BELOW: The '32 Ford roadster, shown here, was perhaps the first example of the modern hot rod because of its torsion rigidity and its ability to handle later produced V-8 engines.

OPPOSITE: A '28 Ford Model A pickup truck.

PAGES 34–35: Another example of the '32 Ford roadster. The owner of this rod added delicate flames over a turquoise paint scheme and chose to keep the fenders.

immense popularity for a variety of reasons. The deuce holds a unique spot in the annals of customized cars. Its history dates to the Model T, which was produced from 1909 to 1927, an extraordinarily long run. Henry Ford was not one to fix something that wasn't broken, but, by the mid-1920s, American tastes had begun to change and sales of the Model T began to falter.

Stutz, Duesenberg, Auburn, and a host of other luxury marques of the era had set a new standard in automotive design. In addition, Ford had transformed the moribund Lincoln into Ford Motor Company's most prestigious line of cars. Clearly, with these changes in the industry, the motoring public hungered for state-of-the-art styling and engineering.

Edsel Ford, long working in the shadow of his famous father, convinced Henry that the Model T's design was dated; at the very least, Edsel felt it needed a facelift. The elder Ford grudgingly agreed and the Model A debuted in 1928. Here was a car that wasn't significantly different from its predecessor, but was just enough of a change to capture the imagination of the motoring public. The lines were more sleek; the cowl blended especially well into the body. It was enough to dramatically increase sales.

The wave of popularity didn't last long, however. In 1932 the styling of the Model A was beginning to show its age. Buyers wanted luxury in their car, even if it was the low-priced Ford. And buyers also wanted some power under the hood. Adding to the chorus demanding change were Ford's competitors. On the horizon was the Chrysler Airflow, which epitomized a vehicle design based on aerodynamics. General Motors let loose a flamboyant designer, Harley Earl, who recruited stylists schooled in industrial design. Henry and Edsel Ford recognized the upcoming threat, and began thinking in the late '20s and early '30s of a car that would include more power and more elegant lines.

Ford's three-window two-door coupe debuted for the 1932 model year. Referred to affectionately as the "Baby Lincoln," it was a masterpiece of industrial design, comfortable and still affordable. Under the hood was what would become one of Ford's biggest legends: the flathead V-8 engine. It was such a stroke of engineering genius that some dealers displayed cars with clear hoods to allow customers an unobscured view of what was underneath.

The deuce coupe was not all looks and power. Its frame possessed substantially greater torsional rigidity than had the Model T or the Model A. And since Fords, beginning in 1932, could be equipped with the optional V-8, it was not difficult to install newer, more powerful V-8s into those earlier models later on.

RIGHT: *The owner of this '32 Ford roadster opted for the "hi-tech" look with aluminum mag wheels.*

FAR RIGHT TOP: *Disc brakes are featured on this '32 Ford roadster with everything chromed from the backing plate to the shock absorbers.*

FAR RIGHT BOTTOM: *The rear transaxle gets special treatment.*

BUILDING THE PERFECT STREET BEAST

The street rod coupe gained its iconoclastic looks from a practical application. Racing on dirt roads or tracks made Swiss cheese out of fenders, so the owners often removed them. This posed a problem in the '33 coupes, which like all Fords were equipped with inner fender panels, the tops of which mated with the bottom of the hood. Since owners removed their fenders—including the inner fenders—for racing, there was no place for the hood to mate. Thus the hoods were eliminated as well. Complementing the fenderless and hoodless appearance

ABOVE *This '32 Ford highboy roadster features the traditional look, with steel rims and the absence of a hood and fenders.*

OPPOSITE: *This highboy offers another look at a traditional approach to the hot rod.*

were a timeless grille and a straight beltline that gave the car a sleek look, especially when the front end was lowered.

The deuce coupe and highboy are placed into two categories. The "traditional" or "nostalgia" cars hark back to the original basic look, which doesn't go past, say, 1970 in customizing and accessories. These cars usually are equipped with Halibrands, painted steel wheels that may have beauty rings or small hubcaps or American Racing torque-thrust five-spoke wheels. The other style is the "high-tech" car, exemplified by Boyd Coddington designs, or "Boydsters." These cars may feature Billet aluminum wheels and radials.

Building a deuce coupe street rod remains an "anything goes" philosophy, but original Ford components are just about impossible to find these days. However, virtually all Ford parts are now reproduced, and a street rod can be 100 percent manufactured with all-new components. Fiberglass bodies can be purchased that look like the real McCoy. Okesters Custom Rods of Reynoldsburg, Ohio, offers a '32 Ford three-window coupe street rod package for less than $4,000. The package includes a fiberglass body with a 3-inch (7.5cm) chopped and filled top, completed floor and firewall with transmission cover, filled cowl, inner and outer doors, door garnish moldings, dashboard, radiator shell, hood, inner and outer trunk lid, front and rear fenders, and running boards.

Notwithstanding the mid-1960s, when custom street rod builders produced some of the most outrageous designs ever

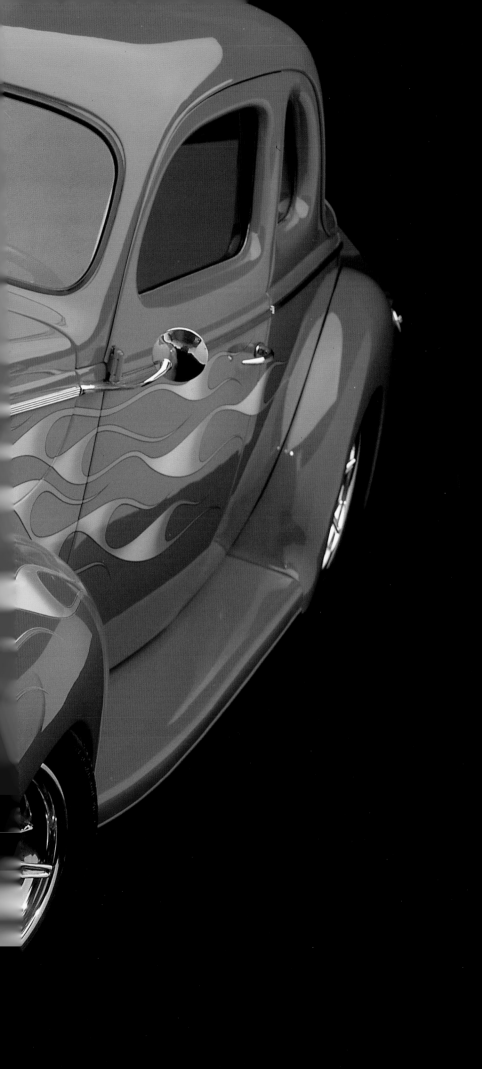

associated with the automobile, street rods are generally built with an emphasis on a clean, uncluttered look. Original body styles are generally left in place, with original or reproduction bumpers, headlamps, trim, and glass remaining on the car. Chopped tops are often the most radical alteration to any street rod. Paint schemes also have emerged from the multicolored phase in the mid-'60s to single colors with perhaps light pin-striping or, at most, flames flowing back from the grille to the doors. Interior and upholstery styling also has become more conservative in the past two decades and selections limited to what the latest luxury factory models have to offer, including leather.

Jaguar front ends in many cases have become the suspension of choice for Ford and Chevy street rods for the superb lightweight construction, handling, ride, and reliability. A 9-inch (23cm) Ford rear end also is a popular component.

Building hybrid cars to marry '90s technology with '40s or '50s styling is the standard approach to building a street machine. Bruce Mollett of Prospect, Kentucky, used a '91 Corvette underneath his '57 Chevy Nomad. It's probably the best example of a high-tech street rod with the panache of the past. Its power started as a Vette 350 small block bored out to 383 cubic inches for 362 horsepower at 5400 rpm to generate 380 pounds-feet of torque at 3800 rpm. The engine also features Silv-O-Lite hyerpeutectic 10.5:1 pistons, Vette D-port aluminum heads, and an Edelbrock TPI manifold. Also installed is an NOS 150-horsepower nitrous oxide setup and Block Hugger headers. Suspension is all Vette as well, with a 3.08:1, 8.5-inch (21.5cm) Dana 44 differential and Vette ZR1 polished rims. So what's left of the Nomad? The frame is all Nomad, but it is modified to accommodate the Vette mechanics. The firewall

LEFT: *The original construction of this '40 Ford coupe is left untouched, but it sports an elaborate flaming paint scheme.*

had been pushed back 6 1/2 inches (16.5cm) and the fender-wells tubbed 3 inches (7.5cm) to make everything fit. The outerskin is virtually all Nomad, with the door handles shaved. Paint is not Chevy but Diamond Porsche rhinestone ruby.

The shoebox Ford also enjoys a resurgence on the street rod scene. A '51 Ford owned by Ron Tegland of Oxnard, California, is also a study in modern technology complemented by design. His Custom Deluxe convertible is powered by a Chevy 454 with stock ported and polished heads, and with Crane valves under Edelbrock valve covers. On top of the Edelbrock manifold is a pair of Holley 750 cfm carbs. All this gives the Ford 550 horsepower at 6500 rpm and 500 pounds-feet at 4500 rpm. A TH400 transmission and B&M 2700 rpm stall torque converter send power to the 4.11:1 gear ratio in a Currie 9-inch rear end. On the outside the front and rear fenders have been extended thanks to parts from a trashed '51 Ford Victoria to allow room for the 454. A new steel hood was fabricated to fit onto the fenders. The body was topped off with DuPont green piping, persimmon scalloped graphics, and a persimmon engine block and accents. VDO liquid-filled gauges, a pair of '57 Buick front seats and RJS harnesses, and a stock Ford rear seat covered in tan leather complete the interior.

OPPOSITE: *Take away the engine treatment and custom wheels and the exterior of this '57 Chevy is virtually stock. Many '55-'57 Chevy owners see little need to customize the graceful lines of these models.*

ABOVE: *The engine of this street rod is all business. It's probably used for straight line racing—if the owner dares to dirty it up a bit.*

LEFT: *The dashboard of this 1957 Chevy Bel Air is stock, but that can't be said for much else. Custom bucket seats, six-point harnesses, and an elaborate console and gauge cluster are sure signs that this vehicle is a serious contender on the track.*

YOU DON'T KNOW WHAT I GOT: STREET ROD POWER

Up until the 1960s, the flathead Ford V-8 and the Hemi engine served as the biggest power plants for street rods. Later, Chrysler 383s, Chevy 427s, and Ford's Boss 429 also served as perfect power plants. As street rods have made a comeback, from the early 1980s through today, many owners have turned to the Chevy 454-cubic-inch engine as their choice for unbridled power. With a compression ratio of 11.25:1 and a Holley Pro-Series HP 750 carb, the 454 can crank 450 horsepower at 5600 rpm and generate as much as 500 pounds-feet of torque. Add custom headers and a custom crankshaft and horsepower is boosted beyond any legal definition of a roadworthy street rod.

Emerging as another source of power is Chevrolet's SB2 engine, designed specifically for NASCAR (National Association for Stock Car Auto Racing). Very few, if any, are found in today's street rods, but early word of this powerful piece of machinery hints that it could very well replace the venerable 454 in the next decade.

The SB2 (and later the SB2.2 engine with an improved head) is a radically designed engine with a new cylinder head that demands much air/fuel mixture be stuffed into each cylinder while using a single 4-barrel carburetor. Not only does this require major alterations to the head but it means that the intake manifold, camshaft, exhaust headers, and other major components must be changed. Still, under NASCAR rules, the SB2 had to be compatible with the existing Chevrolet engine block used in NASCAR races.

Work on the SB2 began in 1993, with the first designs off the board the following year. Prototype testing began in '95, with manufacturing farmed out by General Motors to the leading engine building and racing teams in the country. The compression for this monster was first unlimited, then reduced to 14:1, and then to 12:1.

The SB2 saw track time at the 1998 Daytona, but was still in the testing stage the same year in Michigan, running on a 12:1 compression ratio and unleaded fuel. While its overall speed and performance remain shrouded in secrecy, SB2 engineers anticipate the engine gaining wide popularity.

The SB2 engine points to the ever-changing technology of high-performance engines and the role that they play in street rods and in auto racing in general. While the SB2 is not an engine that is likely to be used for street driving anytime soon, with the proper detuning it will eventually find its way there.

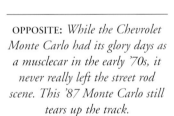

OPPOSITE: *While the Chevrolet Monte Carlo had its glory days as a musclecar in the early '70s, it never really left the street rod scene. This '87 Monte Carlo still tears up the track.*

RIGHT: *Electronic fuel injection and electronic ignition systems are standard equipment on modern factory and custom street rods.*

CHAPTER 2

CUSTOM *RODS*

When one thinks of hot rods, often the first thought is of speed, of powerful, oversized engines tuned for high performance. But many hot rodders are obsessed not with coaxing a few extra horses out of their musclecar engines but with the styling and custom design of their prized cars.

Custom rods are not to be confused with hot or street rods, which feature full racing engines and are built for performance and speed. The custom rods of the '50s rarely had beefed-up engines. In fact, it was a rare thing to have custom rods participate in racing at all, whether on local tracks or a dry lake. But custom rods were often found at these racing venues simply to provide support for the racers, whose interests were limited to such early body styles as fenderless '32 roadsters and coupes. The custom jobs, however— those Mercurys, shoebox Fords, and late-'30s Chevys—were strictly showpieces. They possessed stock engines under the hood and were often chromed for show purposes and fitted with headers for sound.

Competition between customizers and hot rodders was usually good-natured and friendly, but it wasn't uncommon for hot rodders to refer derisively to their custom cousins as "lead-sled" or "low and slow" because the custom cars rarely exceeded cruising speeds on local boulevards. The term lead-sled was somewhat pejorative but became an endearment later for cars that carried up to 100 pounds (45kg) of lead filler that was used to fill seams and holes after chrome trim was removed. It would never have occurred to custom rod owners to actually drive their cars beyond any city, county, or state speed limit. After all, these were cars that had their undercarriages chromed or the trunks and wheelwells fully upholstered. It would be financial suicide to treat such a vehicle as anything other than a showpiece.

Custom emerged not as some elaborate marketing plan but as a simple word-of-mouth movement that ran up and down the California coast. The need was simple. American G.I.s were coming home to warmed-over prewar cars. These 1939 through 1942 models offered a clean industrial look that bored car owners yet were ripe for customization.

PAGE 46: *This '48 Cadillac Sedanette is given the moniker of "Cadzilla" for its elaborate chopped look and heavy custom emphasis.*

PAGE 47: *The dashboard of Cadzilla remains relatively untouched. Note the transmission tunnel custom work.*

OPPOSITE: *A slightly modified '57 Thunderbird (note the minor work on the bumpers) with brushed aluminum mag wheels.*

RIGHT *Custom chrome hubcaps sport the classic Caddy logo.*

CLASSIC POSTWAR CUSTOMS

Brothers George and Sam Barris were already far ahead of the game, having produced customized rods for the public as early as 1941. The Barris boys had been tinkering with Oldsmobile, Chevy, Pontiac, and Cadillac grilles under the Barris Kustom Grilles name. Their use of these "floating grilles" on prewar cars steeped in Detroit industrial design was revolutionary. In 1950 the brothers took a 1940 Mercury and fitted it with a 1948. They blended the rear fenders into the body, skirted the wheelwells, removed the chrome molding, shaved the door handles, and chopped the top. The result was a clean, almost naked and smooth look, uncluttered by the traditional Detroit body accessories.

Another Barris custom job was a '41 Ford owned by Jesse Lopez. It had a '48 Caddy grille installed along with '46 Ford bumpers. It was chopped 4 inches (10cm), with most of the trim and drip molding shaved, the taillamps hand-formed into the bumper guards, and the headlamps frenched. The requisite skirts were added with barely 3 inches (7.5cm) to clear from

pavement to skirt after the rear was lowered. In addition to Caddy hubcaps and wide whitewalls, a metallic forest-green paint job was added.

By the early 1950s any '49–'51 Merc or shoebox Ford would do as a custom project. In fact, most customizers of the era saw these Mercs as perhaps the best vehicle for custom work, especially for chopping the top. An early project was split between the Ayala Brothers body shop in the Los Angeles area and Barris Kustom Grilles. Taking a '49 Merc, the Ayalas performed most of the body work by chopping the top by 4 inches (10cm) and designing fade-away rear fenders. The Barrises installed a Caddy grille, reworked the headlamps, and added the paint. Another '49 Merc was chopped and then had frenched headlamps and fade-away fenders added. The molding was eliminated and the rear taillamps were hidden in the bumper guards or deep in the body to make them appear as tiny as possible. It was a popular trick among customizers but didn't sit particularly well with local law enforcement.

The Hirohata Merc perhaps best exemplifies the development of the customized Mercury and its lasting impression on customizers for the next four decades, not to mention a virtual obsession with Mercs by directors of youth-oriented movies. Bob Hirohata lived in Arcadia, California, but often visited the Barris auto-body shop when it was in nearby Bell. Hirohata owned a chopped '51 Chevy, but became instantly enamored with the Mercury after watching George Barris take a cutting torch to a new one. Hirohata saw the possibilities and went

LEFT: *The '51 Mercury has never lost its popularity in nearly 50 years as a favorite for customizing. The chrome bumpers provide a sharp contrast to a body stripped of its chrome, and to its shaved trunk and door handles.*

PAGE 52–53: *One doesn't think of a '49 Buick Sedanette as a candidate for customizing, but this lowered, chopped, and channeled custom rod is a stunning example of combining the factory design of the horizontal hood portholes and "front teeth" with the owner's custom tastes.*

out and bought himself a used '51. The top was chopped naturally as Barris removed the window frames and "B" pillar, replacing the pillar with side glass. The glass was V-butted and the headlamps were frenched. All trim was shaved and replaced with '52–'53 Buick side trim. It was indeed an extraordinary job, and the car was showcased at the 1952 General Motors Motorama, where it became a sensation among many GM concept cars that were not even running.

In the mid-'50s George Barris got his hands on a '53 Plymouth owned by Ed Sloan. Barris cannibalized a number of Ford grilles and pieced together an extraordinary custom grille shell for Sloan's car. Barris also chopped the top of the Plymouth, performed expert work on frenching the headlamps, and installed a pair of '53 Lincoln taillamps. The frame was lowered and the rear wheelwells graced with scooped skirts, which complemented the side trim that flowed from the door to the rear quarter panel. It was painted a two-tone dark-green metallic and lime mist.

While customizers like the Barris brothers were pioneers in 1950s restyling of Detroit fare, a comparison to today's customizing efforts proves that sometimes nothing changes.

CUTTING-EDGE CUSTOM RODS

Forty-five years later, Troy Trepanier and his father, Jack, had a similar idea. In a custom job for George Poteet, they started with a '54 Plymouth Belvedere body, but similarities with the '50s vintage Mopar end there. Underneath, it's almost all Dodge Viper, the brutish roadster. On the outside the Trepaniers converted the convertible Belvedere to a hardtop, then custom-fabricated the cowl, A-pillars, roof, and glass. The hood was pie-sectioned to 3 inches (7.5cm) toward the front, then shaved of all chrome and reshaped to fit a new windshield and A-pillars. The head- and taillamps are from a Mercedes E320. The grille and front bumper remain from the original '54 Plymouth but are heavily modified.

The Belvedere's wheelbase was shortened from 114 inches to 110 (289.5 to 279.5cm), and the chassis holds Viper front suspension, rear end, and steering box. Under the hood is a '97 Viper GTS 488-cubic-inch V-10 that generates 450 horsepower and 490 pounds-feet of torque. The transmission is a Six-speed Viper/Borg-Warner. Interior wiring, gauges, and steering wheel also are all '97 Dodge Viper. Poteet's Plymouth illustrates the attention paid to the mechanics of custom rods today, and the contemporary desire to put more power under the hood. Still, racing does not factor in custom rod jobs.

Wayne and Margie Jenkins of Cathedral City, California, typify today's custom rod owners. The couple dropped a 426 Hemi into a two-door '48 Ford Anglia but are not interested in testing its mettle on the track. Standing upright and chubby and placed on a 90-inch (228.5cm) wheelbase, the British Angila originally was equipped with a 933-cc 4-cylinder engine that developed a piddling 23 horsepower. The Jenkinses purchased the Anglia in 1990 and already had the Hemi waiting for it. The body remains true to its original styling right down to the bug-eyed headlamps and waterfall grille. But it's all brute underneath. The Hemi has a Billetcrank, steel rods, and electronic fuel injection. To accommodate the elephantine

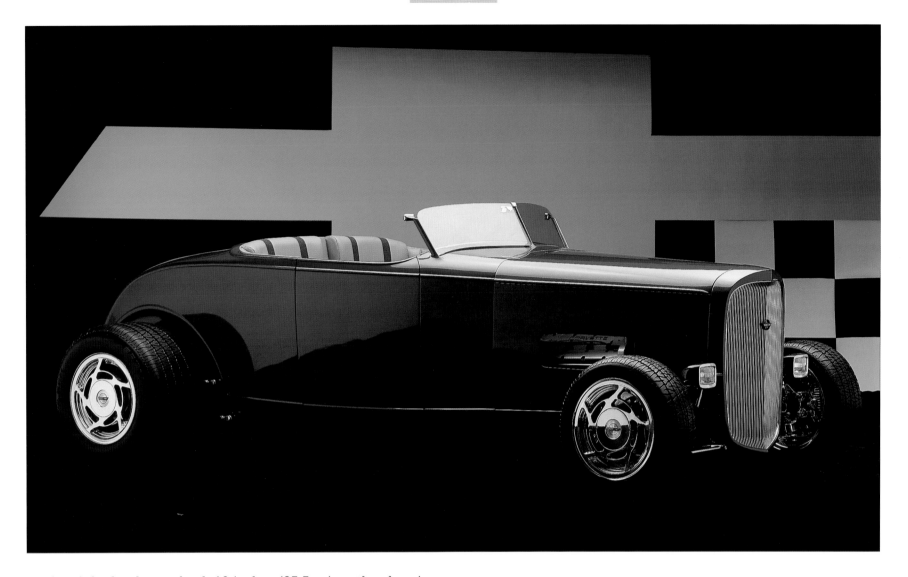

engine, it had to be set back 10 inches (25.5cm) on the chassis, extending the firewall into the interior. Inside are a pair of off-road upholstered bucket seats with four-point seatbelts and a B&M shift kit for the TorqueFlite transmission. A Vega steering box also was installed. While the Jenkinses don't take their British Ford to the track, Wayne Jenkins said he once hit 130 mph (208kph) on the freeway and had plenty of power to spare.

Fred Nicholson lives in Dothan, Alabama, and owns a 1941 Graham four-door Hollywood, a rare custom rod. From the outside, a quick look at this rare bird reveals a Graham that looks suspiciously stock except for the Chrysler 15-inch (38cm) wheels. But under the hood is an '88 340-cubic-inch CI Mopar

OPPOSITE: *A big 427-inch V8 provides plenty of power for a souped-up car, but it's not just power that counts; the engines on the best hot rods are immaculately clean with mirror-like chrome.*

ABOVE: *The only thing retro about this custom rod is the body. Custom wheels, headlamps, and interior complement the body styling and conservative grille.*

engine with a performer intake with Edelbrock carb. The ignition is a Mopar electronic high-performance model with custom dual exhaust and a Mopar 904 transmission to establish a hefty power train.

The frame is stock and the wheelbase remains at 112 inches (285cm). The front suspension, however, is an Aspen torsion bar with Aspen disc brakes in the front and 11-inch (28cm) drums in the rear. The master cylinder, steering box, and column are all Chrysler products. The interior is done up in Light Camel leather upholstery and light-tan carpet. Cadillac power seats are installed in front.

Clyde Moyer's '47 Buick Super convertible is an obvious custom job that also features some hidden strength under the hood. Moyer, of Douglasville, Georgia, had a 455 Buick Stage I engine dropped into the engine compartment. The car also features a 2 1/2-inch (6.4cm) exhaust system with aluminized Brockman Mellowtone Mufflers and a Buick Star Wars air cleaner. The tranny is a 400 Turbo with shift kit. Modifications to the body were extensive. The head- and taillamps were frenched, the side moldings and door handles shaved and decked, the body seams welded and filled, and the front wheel openings flared. The skirts were hand-formed and '53 Plymouth taillamps were installed. The Buick sits on a 127-inch (322.5cm) wheelbase and features 1981 Trans Am front suspension and front disc brakes. The steering column is from an '81 Monte Carlo. The wheels are stock General Motors fare, but with '57 Caddy hubcaps.

Bruce Lingenfelter's '55 Pontiac Star Chief Safari station wagon is a lesson in restraint, balancing perfectly the essence of custom and stock appearance. When Lingenfelter first purchased his Safari it was all stock with an excellent body. He

A '51 Ford convertible custom rod.

completely rebuilt it and drove it before reengineering the front brake system and fitting a 1990 454-cubic-inch SS Chevy truck engine in it and changing the steering to a later model Saginaw 605. The 454 has fuel injection and the ignition is stock. Power is transmitted through a 400 Turbo tranny and modified '55 Pontiac shifter.

The body remains stock (the only custom giveaway is the Centerline wheels and Michelin radials) and is painted a two-tone aqua and black acrylic enamel. The interior features aqua carpet and aqua and black upholstery. The engine compartment was modified to refit the motor mounts to accommodate the 454 and new transmission. It sits on a 122-inch (310cm) wheelbase and its front suspension is still '55 Pontiac but with an SJ Grand Prix modified sway bar, with the rear a narrowed Ford 9-inch (23cm) with stock leafs and added Chevy truck leafs. The front brakes came off a 454 SS Chevy truck, adapted to '55 spindles, and the rear brakes are 11-inch (28cm) drums from a Lincoln.

Another Pontiac belongs to Richard Cortez of Rialto, California. Cortez owns a 1939 Pontiac Chief convertible powered by a 427 big block engine lifted from a '73 Corvette. It features Pontiac valve covers. The top was chopped 3$\frac{1}{2}$ inches (9cm) and dechromed. The door handles were shaved and the license plate was molded into the trunk lid. Despite its power, it's strictly a show car, Cortez says.

These '90s custom jobs exemplify the dramatic changes that custom rodding has gone through over the decades. Sophistication and emphasis not only to the body but the interior, sound system, and engine now play an integral part in the car show of any given custom rod.

RIGHT: *This '55 Chevy sedan had its bumpers integrated into the body but retains its original factory grille. Its owner even left alone the squared wheel openings in the rear.*

PAGES **60–61**: *A classic, custom deuce coupe.*

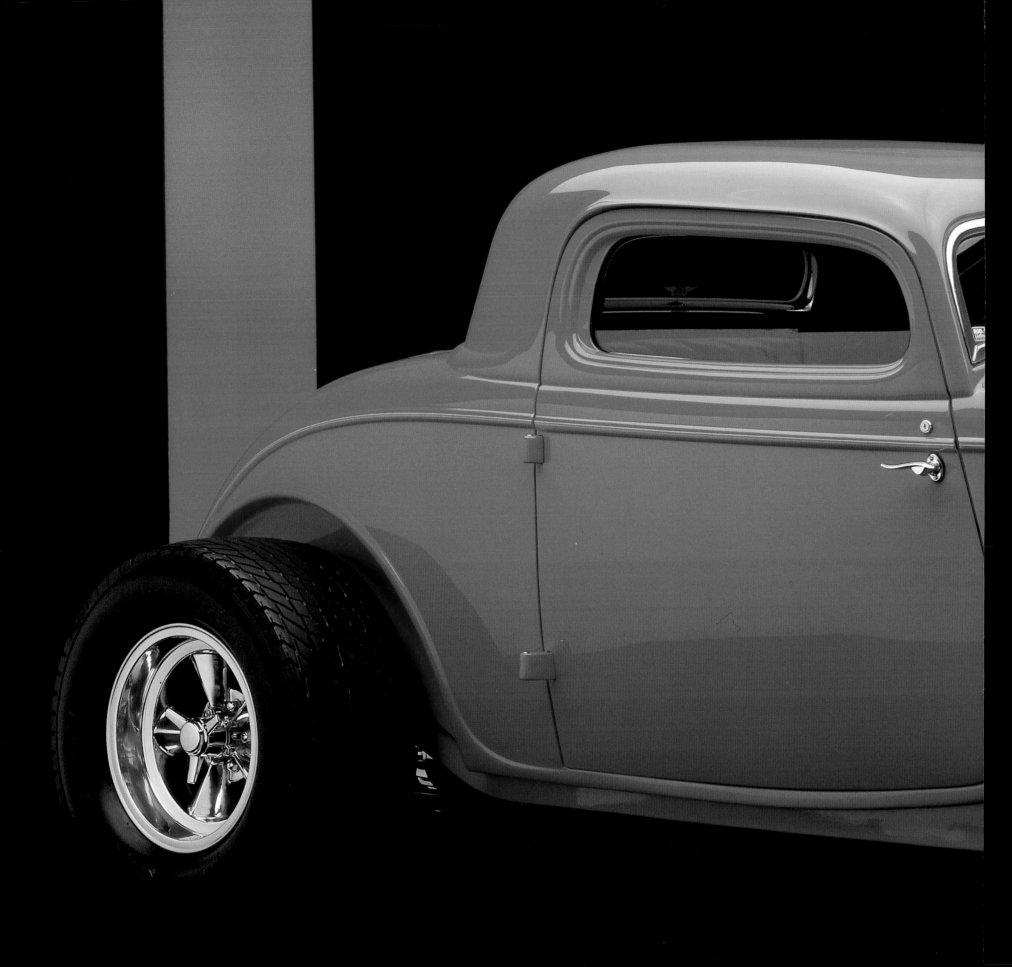

OUTSIDERS AND LOWRIDERS: A WHOLE OTHER CUSTOM ROD

The lowrider phenomenon began as a small movement during the closing months of World War II, as Mexican-American servicemen returned to East Los Angeles. The Mexican-American community of 1945 was profoundly segregated from the rest of Los Angeles. Local newspapers represented young Mexican-American men as hooligans while their girlfriends and wives were depicted as women of questionable morals. There were virtually no recreational activities and what there was had to be segregated from white residents.

Customized cars began to pop up along Whittier Boulevard and other cruise venues, much like other communities. But the difference between, say, custom car owners in Pasadena and those of East Los Angeles was immediately apparent. Here were cars that were lowered to just inches off the pavement, with the rear end nearly dragging along the asphalt and the grille pointed almost skyward. Mercs, Chevy Bel Airs, and Pontiacs ruled cruise nights. Later it was Chevy Impalas and Buick Rivieras.

The appeal of the lowrider had a lot to do with who was driving them. Perhaps for the first time in L.A. history, East Los Angeles children had role models to look to: the military veteran who island-hopped in the Pacific on the way to victory in Tokyo or the citizen soldier who liberated concentration camps in Germany and Poland. Mexican-American veterans, already idolized in their community, were driving way-too-cool cars that often defied description. Compounding the appeal were the inevitable clashes with Los Angeles County sheriff's deputies who attempted in every conceivable way to ticket, if not arrest, the *vato* and impound his ride. While many car clubs had such clashes with the local law, Los Angeles County sheriff's deputies broke up cruises along Whittier Boulevard with particular zeal. They might have won the skirmishes, but the *vato* would win the war. The Mexican-American veteran became a virtual folk hero in his community and his machine a shining trophy to acquire.

When the veterans began attending college on the G.I. Bill, the popularity of the lowrider began to spread to college campuses and to other communities. For many years it remained almost exclusively in the domain of Mexican-Americans. The close-knit cultural custom car hobby didn't significantly break racial barriers until the late 1970s and early '80s, when African-Americans and whites began to appreciate the beauty and uniqueness of the lowrider.

The Chicano movement of the late 1960s and the founding of *Lowrider* magazine laid the groundwork that legitimized the lowrider. Much as *Hot Rod* magazine had served as a voice for the outlaw hot rodder a generation earlier, *Lowrider* captured the spirit of a new type of car enthusiast, one who was somewhat misunderstood by the public at large. But unlike the hot rodders of generations past, lowriders were seeking political expression as much as a venue in which to enjoy their hobby.

"El Larry" Gonzales, David Nunez, and Sonny Madrid were active in the Chicano movement. The three were influenced by *Con Safos,* an East Los Angeles publication that brought together Chicano politics and the lowrider. An early centerfold was a low-slung '47 Chevy on Cragar wheels. With Gonzales in charge of funding new projects, the "Low Rider Associates" began examining gang violence, and organizing political campaigns for Latino candidates.

By 1976 Low Rider Associates was in high gear in sponsoring cruises and other events to raise money. An estimated 8,000 lowriders participated in San Jose Chicano Bicentennial

OPPOSITE, TOP: *This 1961 Chevrolet Nomad station wagon owned by Mario DeAlba Sr., features a three-stage pearl paint job with a metal flake top. The car rides on front and rear hydraulics. (photo by Walt Weiss)*

OPPOSITE, BOTTOM: *Lusi Capilla owns this 1964 Chevrolet Impala Super Sport with a two-tone, two-stage paint scheme, wheel skirts, and front and rear hydraulics. (photo by Walt Weiss)*

on July 3, 1976, which provided seed money for *Lowrider* magazine. Madrid was named publisher and the following year the debut issue of the magazine hit the stands. Mixing social issues with cars drew some criticism, but *Lowrider* flourished. The magazine today remains a powerful voice for Chicanos and their cars, not to mention being the longest-running Chicano publication.

Today's lowriders range from the understated to the whacked out. It is the most personal of any hot rod theme. Unlike musclecars, which fit into a specific make, model, and year of a car, or street rods with an emphasis on deuce coupes and highboys, any car can be customized into a lowrider. These cars can range from a '59 Impala to a '96 Acura. There is no concrete definition of what constitutes a lowrider. If one were to pigeonhole owners into specific themes, then perhaps the older vato would generally be seen in '49–'54 Chevys or Mercs of similar years. Even the occasional early-'50s Cadillac and Packard may be spotted at the show. Sons and daughters of World War II veterans may prefer the late-'50s through early-'70s Chevys and Buicks while today's young turks may be inclined to cherry out Hondas, Acuras, or any number of late-model Detroit models.

CUSTOM CHROME MIRRORED IN DETROIT

There was a point in the early 1960s when the future of custom rods was threatened. Customizing a car was limited only by one's imagination, and, boy, did customizers have wild imaginations. Chrome became the accouterment of the day as customizers heaped more and more shiny stuff on their already sagging, heavy cars. Ironically, this fad followed the hubris displayed by Detroit automakers in the late 1950s, when heavy gobs of chrome were the order of the day. Such heavy-handed styling in effect helped put an end to such distinguished careers as that of Harley Earl, chief stylist for General Motors.

Earl's '58 Buick Century represented everything that was excessive about Detroit cars, with a hodgepodge assortment of chrome molding and heavy bumpers. While the Buick wasn't solely responsible for the end of Earl's reign, it illustrated the changing taste of the buying public and the fact that Earl's vision was obsolete. So it's interesting to note that customizers, in their own individualistic way, followed suit by chroming the most obscure parts of their rods.

By 1962 the tastes of car owners had changed. Cars became more compact and Detroit began to emphasize what was under the hood rather than the exterior styling. The '51 Merc, considered a relic of '50s-era sock hops and drive-in burger stands by some, gave way to the GTO, the Ford Mustang, and the semicompact Chevy. Magazines like *Motor Trend* and *Hot Rod* began to focus more attention on engine modifications. Detroit automakers picked up on the new interest and began offering the 396 and 454 engines. Classic custom rodding took a backseat for a while, but never went completely away. In recent years, it has made a comeback, as evidenced by Nicholson's '41 Graham, Lingenfelter's '55 Pontiac, and Moyer's '47 Buick.

ABOVE: *The front end system of a Boyd Coddington custom rod.*

OPPOSITE: *A '50 Oldsmobile Rocket 88 was a favorite among teens in the 1950s and remains a classic today with this custom treatment.*

MUSCLE *CARS*

Performance became the goal in the late '50s and early '60s, as styles and tastes evolved among enthusiasts. Engines got progressively bigger, and could be swapped and modified more affordably. Gone were the venerable Chevy Stovebolt 6 and 6-cylinder flatheads. V-8s had been around since 1932, but it wasn't until about 1949 that serious thought was given to adding significant horse-power and torque to enhance performance.

Detroit tapped into the youth market in a big way in the early '60s. Baby boomers were now of driving age and wanted something more than chrome and slow cruises along the local strip. They wanted power. The thought in the mid-'60s was that a short rear deck cut off the air flow more quickly, thereby boosting speed. Thus was born a new style of car, with longer, flatter hoods and a short deck. The Chevy Monte Carlo, not a typical musclecar (although it could be ordered with the leg-endary factory-equipped 454-cubic-inch engine), had a hood the size of the top deck of an aircraft carrier and a rear deck barely big enough to lay out a road map. There was a sexiness to the muscle styling and performance engine not found in the lead-sleds of the '50s.

To appreciate the roots of the musclecar one must go back to the 1930s, and the advent of the V-8 engine. Two power plants in particular deserve credit for sowing the seeds of hi-po driving: the Ford flathead V-8 and Chrysler's Hemi engine. Ford got its start in 1932, while Chrysler had tinkered with the V-8 until 1951.

FORD'S FLATHEAD V-8: THE GRANDDADDY OF MUSCLE ENGINES

While Ford flathead V-8s are rarely found in today's street machines or musclecars, the engine bridges, along with the Hemi, past and present technology. It bears discussion since it serves as the granddaddy of engines for performance vehicles. Ford introduced the flathead V-8 in March 1932 after Ford engineers Emil Zoerlein, Ray Laird, and Carl Schultz worked in secret to produce what many thought was impossible to build successfully: a 90-degree V-8. Primitive technology created cracks, casting pinholes, and overheating in early flathead V-8s. But the trio's efforts finally resulted in an engine that featured a single belt, a generator/fan combination, two water pumps, a Detroit Lubricator carburetor, and an aluminum intake manifold. Water to cool the engine entered the heads at top center. The first version had a displacement of 221 cubic inches with a bore and stroke of 3.0625 x 3.750 inches (7.78 x 9.53cm) and a compression ratio of 5.5:1 to generate 65 horsepower at 3400 rpm. Two years later, a new Stromberg dual-downdraft carb boosted performance another 10 horsepower.

PAGE **66:** *The 1968 Camaro Super Sport is considered perhaps the most desirable musclecar of the late '60s and early '70s generation of street monsters. The SS package came loaded with options including the 396- and 454-cubic-inch V-8 engines.*

PAGE **67:** *Instrument cluster on the Boss Mustang.*

RIGHT: *The '67 Ford Mustang GTA convertible featured a modest stock 289-cubic-inch V-8.*

By 1939 six million flathead V-8s had been built. A 239.4-cubic-inch bored-out version with a 6.3:1 compression ratio for 95 horsepower was dropped into Mercurys. Ford cars got the 239 after World War II. The 336-cubic-inch engine debuted in 1948 and was sold exclusively with F-7 and F-8 trucks. The following year saw Ford's Lincoln line get an even more improved version of the 336, with 152 horsepower over the 145 horsepower of the previous year's trucks.

The model year 1949 was important both to Ford and to street-machine owners as a slightly modified version of the 336 flathead V-8 was installed in Mercurys. The Mercury's body was always ripe for modifications—both prewar and postwar stylings—but coupled with the new streamlined look came an engine that could conceivably blow the doors off the competition at any boulevard stoplight. The Mercury engine had a bore and stroke of 3.50 x 4.38 inches (8.9 x 11.1cm) for 145 horsepower and 225 pounds-feet of torque. The bellhousing was no longer cast as part of the engine block and the oil pump was converted to a shorter, more straight-cut gear pump to provide higher oil pressure. The intake and exhaust systems were improved and the distributor was modernized and relocated above the front of the right side of the cylinder bank. The fan pitch, cam, and exhaust were modified to make less noise. There was a modified, but mild, cam installed as well, although the later '49s and models through 1951 sported cams more suitable for racing.

The model year 1953 was the last year for Ford's flathead V-8. But the engine has endured among hot rodders. It continues to be popular not because its technology remains competitive with today's high-tech engines; hardly, as these engines are at least forty-five years old. They remain popular today because they provide adequate horsepower, can be modified easily for bigger output, and simply because they are cool and different to have.

OPPOSITE: *The '70 "Boss 302" is probably considered the finest Mustang ever designed and engineered next to the 1965 Shelby Mustang. The Boss 302 offered a slightly modified fastback treatment and a deluxe racing package.*

ABOVE: *A Shelby 302-cubic-inch V-8 belonging to a '70 Boss Mustang. It features 290 horsepower at 5800 rpm with a four-barrel Holley carb.*

CHRYSLER'S LEGENDARY HEMI: THE BACKBONE OF MOPAR MUSCLE

While Ford made steady improvements with its V-8, Chrysler was saddled with its L-head Six and Straight Eights, even in the early postwar years. Chrysler engineers James C. Zeder, M. L. Carpentier, and W. E. Drinkard spent most of those early postwar years developing a new engine that was designed in such a way that would provide for free-breathing ports and low compression ratio to allow the engine to run on low octane fuel. Ultimately, drag racers would modify the Hemi engine to obtain as much as 1,000 horsepower.

The Hemi was a complicated engine, and therefore a costly one to produce. Its interchangeable heads alone were heavy and expensive to build. Extensive modifications to later, larger Hemis forced engineers to make the engine taller to accommodate longer connecting rods, designating them as the "raised block" or "tall deck" Hemis. So it was a risk for Chrysler to invest resources and money into a project that could fail.

The first Hemi to debut was the Firepower V-8 in 1951. It only hinted at things to come. Dropped into the Saratoga and the higher-priced New Yorker, the extended block Hemi had a 331-cubic-inch displacement and a 3.81-inch (9.7cm) bore and 3.63-inch (9.2cm) stroke. It generated 180 horsepower at 4000 rpm. Its compression ratio was 7.5:1. Saddled with a Carter 2-barrel carb, its output was modest.

Still, the 331 was not about to be dismissed. A Saratoga equipped with a stock Hemi—which conceivably was semicompetition transportation—could hit 60 mph (96kph) from a standstill in 10 seconds and reach a top speed of 110 mph (176kph). Not bad in 1951. Bill Sterling captured first place in his class driving a 331 Saratoga at the '51 Mexican Road Race and came in third overall behind a pair of Ferraris. Four special Hemis derived from the 331 were built to achieve 400 horsepower for the 1953 Indianapolis 500.

As far as street use was concerned, the 331 was hampered by an extension behind the block to house a fluid couple unit for the Fluid Torque Drive automatic transmission. The transmission was poor, and it was replaced in 1954 when horsepower was boosted to 235 by using a Carter 4-barrel carb and enlarging the exhaust ports. The 331s remained on the New Yorker and the New Yorker Deluxe, but the engine really proved itself in 1955 with the introduction of Chrysler's famed 300 letter-series car. The first one, the C-300, was equipped with a new compression ratio of 8.5:1, thanks to the availability of high-octane fuels. It now featured a pair of 4-barrel carbs that finally showed the motoring public what a Hemi could really do. Horsepower was now ranked at 300 at 5200 rpm (hence the name 300) with 345 pounds-feet of torque at 3200 rpm.

In 1956 the 354 Hemi was dropped into a New Yorker with a 9:1 compression ratio and a larger bore and stroke of 3.94 x 3.63 inches (10.0 x 9.2cm). Horsepower was initially 280 with a 4-barrel carb for the New Yorker, but the Chrysler 300B saw its pony power jump dramatically to 340 at 5200 rpm with dual 4-barrel carbs, a special cam, and mechanical lifters. An optional 354 for the 300B offered 355 horsepower, dual 4-barrel carbs,

PAGE 72: *The Plymouth 'Cuda, special edition Chevrolet Camaro Yenko, and the Mustang were the premier musclecars of the late 1960s and early '70s, back before safety and smog regulations sapped their power.*

PAGE 73: *Ram scoop of a '70 Plymouth 'Cuda.*

and a 10:1 compression ratio. The 300B could achieve 0–60 mph (96kph) in 8.2 seconds, with a top speed of 135 mph (216kph).

For the model years 1957 and '58, Chrysler brought in the raised block Hemi, a 392-cubic-inch street monster with an even bigger bore and stroke of 4.0 x 3.9 inches (10.2 x 9.9cm) for 375 horsepower for the 300C. The '58 300D saw its horsepower boosted to 380 with dual 4-barrel carbs, and with fuel injection the 300D enjoyed a 390-horsepower rating.

The Hemi reached its pinnacle with the 392 engine, but in the end it proved too expensive to build. Its 1951–58 life span is relatively short for an engine. Chrysler replaced it with the wedge-shaped 383-cubic-inch V-8 in 1959, which achieved its own following in the automaker's B-series engines. The Hemi would return in 1964 in the form of the elephantine 426, debuting at the 1964 Daytona 500. Richard Petty, driving a Belvedere equipped with a '64 Race Hemi, captured first place, and four of the top five finishers in that race were Chrysler products powered by the 426 Hemi. For very much the same reasons the Ford flathead V-8 was so popular—its uniqueness, solid power, and link to the past—the Hemi has enjoyed a continued life in street machines being built today.

THESE PAGES: *The 1964 Plymouth Hemi was a favorite among factory lightweight racing fans in the mid- and late-1960s. The spartan styling both inside (opposite) and out (below) one belies the power under its hood.*

BIG BAD MUSCLECARS OF THE '60S

Perhaps the most popular street machines on the road during the early- and mid-1960s were the 409 Chevy Impala SS and the Pontiac Grand Prix. The '55–'57 Chevys were street icons, often equipped with the 409. Later on, the 396 and 454s were dropped in for no-nonsense, full-throttle power.

The '63 406 Ford Galaxie XL also left its mark on early street machines. The Galaxie was Ford's answer to the Mercury Marauder and Max Wedge Dodges and Plymouths as one of the hottest cars on the racetrack and on the street. The fastback Galaxie, sometimes called a "scatback" or "slant-

back," debuted in January 1963. The 406 Galaxie was a precursor to the 427s. All Galaxies were to be fitted with the 427, which would garner a lot of attention in the automotive press in the mid-'60s when raced by Dan Gurney and Fred Lorenzen. But the 406 Galaxie—only 136 were factory built—points to a brief shining moment for the 1962 model year when Ford was pitted against similar-sized Chevys, Dodges, and Pontiacs.

BELOW: *A rare example of a 1961 Chevrolet Impala "Bubble Top." Nearly 200,000 hardtop sports sedans were built, but few survived as musclecars or hot rods.*

As Ford geared up to produce its 427 Galaxies, it used its existing inventory of 406s from the previous model year before discontinuing its use in production cars in early 1963. The 427 was essentially a bored-out 406. The 406 possessed a 4.13-inch (10.5cm) bore and 3.78-inch (9.6cm) stroke for 405 horsepower at 5800 rpm and a torque of 448 pounds-feet at 3500 rpm, and it hit 60 mph (96kph) from a dead stop in 7 seconds. With the 427, the bore and stroke measured 4.23 x 3.78 inches (10.7 x 9.6cm) with a 11.5:1 compression ratio, a Holley 4-barrel carb to offer 410 horsepower at 5600 rpm. In 1963 fifty Galaxies with the 427 (at 425 horsepower) were built as factory lightweights.

The Impala SS 409 could easily outpace the Ford Galaxie (from 0–60 in 6.3 seconds) with a slightly higher horsepower of 409 at 6000 rpm and torque rated at 420 pounds-feet at 4000 rpm. A Dodge 330, on the other hand, could rate 385 horsepower at 5200 rpm and provide 455 pounds-feet of torque at 3600 rpm from its 413-cubic-inch engine. The Pontiac Grand Prix's numbers are not much different than the Galaxie's, with its 421-cubic-inch engine offering 405 horses at 5600 rpm and 425 pounds-feet of torque at 4400 rpm.

Perhaps the most popular musclecars on the road as the '60s drew to a close were the 1968–72 Chevrolet Chevelles. The models featured 396-, 427-, and 454-cubic-inch engines. Chevrolet followed on the heels of Dodge and Ford by introducing its first intermediate car in 1964. The Chevelle was received well by the motoring public, and got an even bigger boost with a redesign in 1966 that shook off some of its economy-car styling but also made it a larger car. And in 1968 Chevy followed again with a major redesign that virtually abandoned the old square-lined look and gave the Chevelle flowing contours that would forever identify it as a General Motors product. The musclecar of choice, at least for Chevy lovers, was the Chevelle SS (Super Sport) 396, which had been around since 1966, and later the 454. In 1968 the SS 396 convertible and Sports Coupe sported a black-out grille, rockers, and back

ABOVE: *The calling card of many muscle cars is the modified V-8 engine, stuffed beneath a long, flat hood.*

panel, red-stripe tires to top off a slight racing image, and a domed hood to give a hint of the massive power underneath. The Super Sports could be ordered with optional bucket seats and center console.

For the 1968–69 models the 396 engine featured a bore and stroke of 4.09 x 3.76 inches (10.4 x 9.6cm), with horsepower rankings at 325, 350, and 375 depending on the compression ratio and carburetion. For 1970–72 the 402-cubic-inch engine was used. But the buyer got a tad bigger engine. Chevy didn't want to monkey with the "396" badge because of its popular identity. The bore was enlarged to 4.13 inches (10.5cm) with horsepower at a modest 240 or 300, 350, and 375. For the 1970–72 model years, the 454 provided a bore and stroke of 4.25 x 4.00 inches (10.8 x 10.2cm), with its most powerful engine ranked at 450 horsepower at 5600 rpm. These huge

RIGHT: *A 1970 Chevrolet Chevelle Super Sport powered by an LS6 V-8 454-cubic-inch Turbo-Jet engine that generates 450 horsepower.*

OPPOSITE: *The top dog of factory-built Chevy engines, the 454.*

monsters could offer as much as 500 pounds-feet of torque at 3600 rpm with a 11.25:1 compression ratio and a 4-barrel carb.

Even with such unadulterated power, there are enthusiasts who just aren't happy unless they can give their muscle-car just a little bit more under the hood. Doug Prince of California owns a '69 Camaro Rally Sport Z/28 that has all the outward appearances of your standard factory-issued RS Z/28, complete with vinyl roof, Rally wheels, and cowl induction hood. The surprise lurks underneath. Prince dropped a 468-cubic-inch big block engine with a 13:1 compression ratio. The crankshaft is stock Chevy but it's moved by TRW pistons and polished Chevy 3/8 rods. The engine breathes through a set of polished and ported square-port, open-chamber heads with 2.19-inch (5.6cm) intake and 1.88-inch (4.8cm) exhaust stainless valve springs. The power is transferred through a B&M Turbo 400 tranny and Wenco driveshaft to a 12-bolt rear end and 4.33:1 gearing. At a quarter mile it clocks 11.49 with a top speed of 119 mph (190kph). Beyond the occasional drags and cruises, this puppy doesn't get much driving time—it averages about four miles (6.5km) a gallon.

Being part of the musclecar crowd doesn't necessarily mean that the enthusiast must neatly fit into the musclecar mold. A '62 Chevy Nova owned by Pro Streeter Mark Grimes belies what one would expect from a car that was originally conceived as an economy car. Grimes's Nova is powered by a stock '87 Chevy 4.3-liter V-6 that features headers and a B&M air cleaner. This jackrabbit is powered through a Currie 9-inch (23cm) rear end with 3.70:1 gears to a set of Goodrich tires on 17 x 12 Boyds Posies inside huge 34-inch (86cm) tubs. Like Prince's Camaro, the body remains intact and virtually stock, with the exception of a deep-pearl-green Ditzler paint job and tan leatherette upholstery for the seats.

The SS 396 and SS 454 and Rally Sport Camaros might have been a toy for the young male of the late '60s and early '70s, but it could be one bad toy if it was in the wrong hands. This was a huge engine in a relatively light 3,600-pound (1,600kg) car on a 112-inch (285cm) wheelbase. The 325-horsepower version of the 396 had a mild cam but a hefty low-end torque that would allow the car to hit a shade over 13 seconds in a quarter-mile run. Tie together the engine and not-too-sharp handling with a four-speed close-ratio Muncie tranny and many a novice driver found himself wrapped around a tree. Detroit automakers must take a share of the blame for such awesome power. Chevy's performance options—and those of the other Detroit car manufacturers as well—emphasized straight-line performance with little offered in the way of improved handling. The suspension and overall handling of the Chevelle SS didn't measure up to the power.

Challenging Chevy but not reaching true appreciation by enthusiasts until 1970 was the Oldsmobile 4-4-2. Oldsmobile wanted an answer to its sister division Pontiac's GTO. The 4-4-2, which stands for 4-barrel carburetor, four on the floor, and dual exhaust pipes, graced Olds' showroom floors in 1964, but the cars came in too late to be properly marketed to young drivers. Still, Oldsmobile was no Johnny-come-lately to the musclecar game. It had produced the Rocket 88, which rivaled the Chrysler Hemis in the early 1950s. The Rocket won more than half the NASCAR races during the organization's first three seasons. And it was the engine of choice for dragsters hitting 150 mph (240kph) in a quarter mile.

For a mere $136 above the sticker price, the 4-4-2 package could be installed on any F-85 or Cutlass, except for the station wagon. The engine had a heft to it but nothing to go gaga over. The Jetfire Rocket V-8 displaced 330 cubic inches for 290 horsepower at 520 rpm and reasonable torque at 355 pounds-feet at 3600 rpm. Oldsmobile went all out for the 1965 model year, including the 4-4-2 in its catalog and a small supplement devoted exclusively to the 4-4-2's features. What impressed buyers the most, however, was the improved engine. It now displaced 400 cubic inches with 345 ponies under the hood and

LEFT: *Interior of a '62 Chevrolet Nova.*

OPPOSITE: *This '62 Chevy Nova pro streeter, owned by Mark Grimes, is powered by an '87 Chevy 4.3-liter V-6 with a B&M air cooler. It's powered through a Currie 9-inch rear end with 3.70:1 gears to a set of Goodrich tires on 17 x 12 Boyds Posies inside huge 34-inch tubs.*

an impressive, tree-trunk-pull torque of 440 at 3200 rpm. The 400 rivaled the early Galaxie 409 and Dodge Hemis, clocking in at 7.1 seconds in 0–60 mph and 15.5 seconds with a top speed of 91 mph (146kph) in the quarter-mile sprint. It would serve Olds well through 1969, with varying horsepower ranging from 290 to 360.

In 1967 the rare and highly collectible W30 package on the 4-4-2 made its entry. The W30 package provided an outside air-induction system, a trunk-mounted battery, a special cam and valve springs, and an effort to slightly dress up the sizable engine with chrome valve covers. The 4-4-2 reached its pinnacle with the 1970 W30 version, with its bolder split grille, die-cast W30 front fender badges, and wide white racing stripes for the hood. And that was just the pretty stuff. Under the hood was the biggest factory engine ever put in a piece of Detroit iron. Now displacing 455 cubic inches with a full bore of 4.13 inches (10.5cm) and a 4.25-inch (10.8cm) stoke, the V-8 ponied up 370 horsepower and a brutal 500 pounds-feet of torque at 3600 rpm. Oldsmobile also was conscious of weight as an enemy of good performance. The 455 weighed less than the 400, and a W25 package added a fiberglass Ram-Air hood; a W27 version provided an aluminum rear axle carrier.

The model year 1970 proved to be Oldsmobile's last serious foray into the musclecar arena. For 1971 it continued with the 455, but its compression ratio was dropped from 10.5:1 (offered since 1966) to a modest 8.5:1. Horsepower subsequently dropped to 340 or 350, depending on the package.

New body styling from Chevrolet gave the 1969 Camaro Z28 a longer and lower look. The Z28 package came with dual exhaust, special front and rear suspension, Quick-Ratio steering, Rally wheels and a hefty 302-cubic-inch V-8 engine that generated 350 horsepower.

THESE PAGES: *The 1970 Dodge Challenger was
Dodge's answer to the Camaro and Mustang.
It was offered as a two-door hardtop (above), or
a convertible. Power options included the 440 in
the RT versions (opposite).*

GOING OUT WITH A WHIMPER: THE END OF THE MUSCLECAR ERA

The 4-4-2 remained until 1980, but by then it was a shadow of its former self, as federal emission standards and a fuel crisis in 1973 all but sapped its power. It was revived in 1985 but it never recaptured the mystique and brutal power that it once possessed.

The Mopar camp has probably offered more in the way of near limitless power with its emphasis on engineering since the first days after World War II. It hit its stride with the Hemi, but its B engines also served the musclecar driver well, with the 340 as well as 383 engines in its Dodge Charger and Challenger and Plymouth 'Cuda.

The Charger debuted in 1966 as part of the '60s fastback craze. It was boxy, a bit awkward, and placed on the Coronet chassis. While sales for the '66 Charger were good, with more than 37,000 rolling out of the showroom, sales were less than half that for '67. Still, there was no denying that Dodge offered more choices in large engines than any of its competitors. The 361 offered a modest horsepower output of 265, then the 383 with either a 2-barrel or 4-barrel carb. Next came the 426 Hemi with 4-barrel carburetion, or the 426 Street Hemi with horsepower ranges up to 425. A 440 Wedge that had a more modest horsepower output of 375 at 4400 rpm could also be had in the Charger. Sales jumped dramatically to 96,100 for both the completely restyled standard-issue Charger and the high-performance R/T (for Road and Track) model. The R/T no doubt got a tremendous punch in sales when it was featured racing the streets of San Francisco against a Mustang in the Steve McQueen film *Bullitt*.

The musclecar era and the accompanying fascination with the funny car on the drag strip in the 1960s and '70s cemented the hot rod hobby's emphasis on cutthroat power. Even today, with custom rod owners and lowriders who put the accent on styling and appearance, a big engine is necessary to complement the rest of the car. The musclecar era had a little something to do with that.

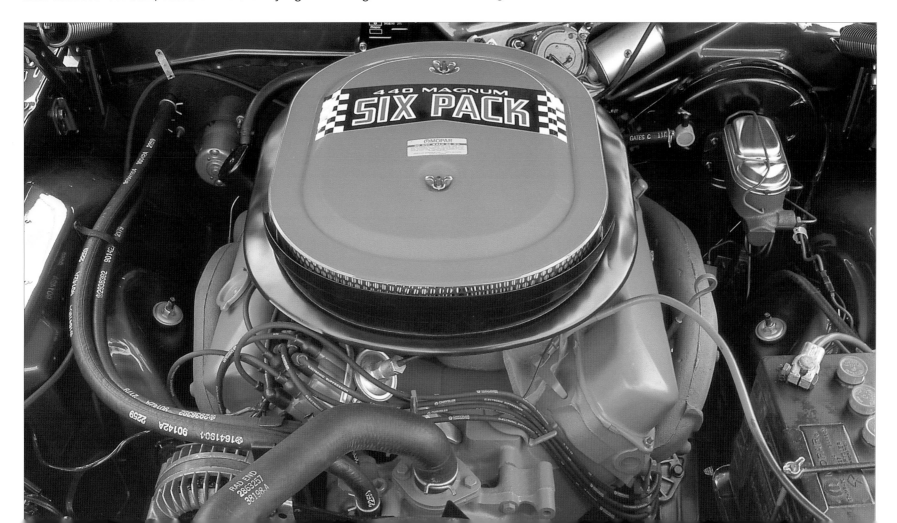

CHAPTER 4

FACTORY *RODS*

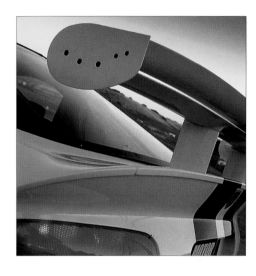

Since the early years of automobiles, automakers understood that performance on the racetrack meant a boost in sales. Bragging rights were sought by the best: first by Duesenberg, Stutz, and Mercer, and later on by Chevrolet, Ford, and Chrysler. Pike's Peak, Daytona, Sebring, and the Bonneville Salt Flats became the proving grounds where automakers could post fast times and endurance records. These records could then be exploited by Madison Avenue advertising agencies, who translated the stats into sales.

Automakers soon began building their own cars and putting them on the track. These racers were high-performance rods detuned for the public or factory lightweights—the kissing cousin of the musclecar, found on drag strips and stock car racetracks. The factory lightweights were produced in limited numbers for the public to satisfy Super Stock racing rules. If Detroit automakers were not building their own special brand of car, the task was often farmed out to independents, who put their own spin on existing models.

CARROLL SHELBY BUILDS A BETTER MUSTANG

Carroll Shelby, a Texas-born, chili-loving race driver, was one such independent car maker. The father of the legendary AC Cobra, Shelby gained instant fame plunking a Ford 260—and, later, 289s and 427s—into a British AC Ace body in the early- and mid-'60s. The result was a howling, brutish machine that trounced Corvettes on the racetrack. Today, original AC Cobras command six-figure prices. Through the late '60s Shelby continued his relationship with Ford by producing the Shelby-American Mustang GT-350, a car that was a Ford in every way except that it was equipped with a special performance package that met Sports Car Club of America (SCCA) production class rules.

The standard 1965 Mustang debuted on April 17, 1964, and gained instant success, much of it thanks to an elaborate and innovative marketing campaign that captured the attention of a young motoring public. The Mustang was the first of the so-called ponycars, with its long hood, short deck, bucket seats, floor shifter, and a relatively large V-8 under the hood. Between its introduction and the end of 1965 model year, 681,000 Mustangs were sold.

To further increase sales, Ford turned to Shelby to produce a racing version of the Mustang. Shelby was required to produce one hundred special Mustangs by January 1, 1965, to meet SCCA rules. To fulfill the requirements, Shelby had Ford's San Jose assembly plant roll out a hundred cars over a two-day period. These cars were all fastbacks with black interiors, four-speed trannys, and 289-cubic-inch engines. The cars came

PAGE 86: *This '63 Shelby Cobra powered by a 289-cubic-inch V-8 Ford engine is a prime example of a hybrid, factory-built car that marries the styling of the AC Ace sports car and an American powerplant.*

PAGE 87: *The Chrysler Corp. developed the beastly Dodge Viper that rivals any European sports car on the road.*

OPPOSITE: *This Shelby Cobra, specially built for racing purposes only, trounced Chevrolet-sponsored Corvettes through most of the 1960s.*

ABOVE: *The spartan interior of the Shelby Cobra. Vibration and engine heat provide for a grueling workout during a long summer's drive.*

RIGHT: *The 427 Cobra was the most powerful Shelby product made for street purposes.*

without hoods, rear seats, exhaust systems, grille bars, or chrome badges. At Shelby's Venice, California, plant, he modified the 289s with beefed-up cranks and rods and aluminum high-riser manifolds. On top was a 4-barrel Holley 715-cfm carb. It had a compression ratio of 11.6:1 to generate 306 braking horsepower at 6000 rpm. He added his own badging, fiberglass hood, and exhaust system.

The engine was also equipped with a baffled 6 1/2-quart (6.2l) cast aluminum oil pan. Its interior baffles prevented oil from sloshing around when the car cornered hard. A Borg Warner T-10 four-speed transmission was the same lightweight gearbox used in Cobras. The Mustangs were painted white with the now-trademark blue racing stripes down the center. No other colors were available. Shelby claimed his Mustang GT 350 could hit 60 mph (96kph) in 5.7 seconds and race from 0–100 mph (160kph) in 14.9 seconds, but none of the automotive magazines that tested them could match those numbers. *Car and Driver* magazine could manage only 6.5 seconds to 60 mph, though that's still not a bad time for a production car.

For the 1966 model year, Shelby toned down the Mustang GT. Some buyers complained about the Detroit Locker limited slip differential, which made a loud cracking noise during cornering and downshifting. It was part of the racing mystique that identified it as a high-performance vehicle, but the average car buyer wasn't ready for it. The Detroit Locker became an option for the 1966 model year and a more quiet exhaust system was installed. Shelby also created a special fleet of GT 350s for the Hertz rental car company, building 936 GT350H models that are now desirable collectibles.

For 1967, the GT 350 had a 328-cubic-inch engine installed to boost horsepower to 355. A special GT 500 version also was offered, with a 428 that was originally found on Cobras. The '67 versions now had a hood air scoop and air scoops installed on the rear quarter panels above the rear wheelwells. The grille was removed to accommodate a pair of high-beam lights. Long rectangular taillamps replaced the triple-light versions.

The Shelby Mustang GT 350 and GT 500 were built through the 1970 model year, although the final year's cars were actually leftover 1969 models that were given 1970 serial numbers. About 14,500 Shelby Mustangs were produced altogether, but Shelby had stepped down from supervising production in 1968, leaving Ford to manage production for the last two years. As a consequence of Shelby's departure, later models were loaded down with creature comforts and were heavier than the high-performance models that Shelby had envisioned when he began the project in 1965.

Another Ford that gained racing fame in its own right and is considerably more desirable among musclecar enthusiasts is

the '69 Boss 429 Mustang. Ford produced the car out of its
Dearborn, Michigan, plant and then farmed out the custom
work to Kar-Kraft of Brighton, Michigan. Though powered by
a 429-cubic-inch engine that was rated at 375 horsepower at
5200 rpm, it is considered to generate a whole lot more ponies
than the official horsepower rating. Torque was rated at 450
pounds-feet at 3400 rpm. Factory-installed heavy-duty suspension and extra sound deadener were added to handle this
big brute.

As musclecars came onto the racing scene in the mid-
1960s, Detroit automakers began producing stripped-down,
high-powered factory lightweights—either building them on

ABOVE: *The 1968 Shelby Mustang GT 500 lost
some of its spunk as buyers of the 1965-66 models
complained that it was too race-oriented and not
driver-friendly. Still, its design and performance
remain contemporary.*

PAGES **92-93**: *1970 Boss Ford Mustang was a
slightly revised version of the '69 model, and offered
many power options.*

their own or farming out jobs to such independent builders as Dearborn Steel Tubing Co. or Automotive Products Co.—to race for the National Hot Rod Association (NHRA) Winternationals. Ford, Chevrolet, Plymouth, Dodge, Pontiac, and Mercury battled one another on the drag strip with cars that had many essential steel parts replaced with aluminum and fiberglass to reduce weight (in many cases, holes were drilled into the frame to further reduce weight), while stock engines were tuned to provide the maximum horsepower.

A '62 Plymouth 420-horsepower 413 Wedge with Tom Grove behind the wheel was the first Super Stock drag-race car to break the 12-second barrier, with a 11.93-second clocking at 118.57 mph (190.78kph).

MOPAR MUSCLE HITS THE STRIP

Mopar dominated the drag strip so much during the early- and mid-1960s with its "Max Wedge" Plymouths that Ford bowed out of drag racing for a while to look for a better car to compete. The Plymouth 426 Max Wedge generated engines with either 415 or 425 horsepower. Dodge was building factory lightweights out of its Hamtramck, Michigan, assembly plant. These cars had the battery mounted in the trunk for better traction and had sound-deadening material, radios, heaters, backseats, sun visors, and other nonessential material removed to make the car as light as possible. Door windows were replaced with Plexiglas and, in some cases, aluminum body panels were installed. These weight-reduction measures shaved as much as 300 pounds (135kg) off the car.

The Dodge "Maximum Performance" 426-ci/425-hp engine was named the "Race Hemi" and enjoyed tremendous popularity. The Race Hemi Dodge was equipped with aluminum fenders and inner fenders, aluminum hood and front bumper, a sparse interior, and a pair of racing bucket seats. Only 271 Race Hemis were manufactured, but anyone with $4,000 could buy one.

Pontiac also recognized early on that a strong performance on the track sold cars, and was the first off the line, producing factory lightweights as early as 1957. In 1961, its best performing car was the Catalina Super-Duty 389 (368 horsepower). A year later the 421-ci/405-hp Catalina hit the track, with its extensive use of aluminum body parts. Pontiac racing great Jim Wangers reached a quarter mile in 12.38 seconds for a top speed of 116.23 mph (187.01kph) at the Detroit Dragway.

Pontiac issued some Catalinas with "Swiss cheese" frames—frames that had holes drilled in them to lighten them up—and achieved a quarter-mile speed of 11.91 seconds before General Motors pulled all of its cars from competition in January 1963.

CHEVROLET STEPS IN

Despite its innovative efforts to shave as much weight as possible from its cars, Pontiac often found itself playing second fiddle to Chevrolet during the early years of Super Stock drag racing. Chevrolet had several advantages, the first of which was that its Bel Air weighed far less than the Catalinas. And while Pontiac had the bigger engines, Chevrolet put the 409-cubic-inch V-8 into the Bel Air—the 360-horsepower engine helped Chevy capture the Top Stock Eliminator title at the NHRA Winternationals.

In 1962 the Z-11 package debuted, using extensive aluminum parts and a 409 engine now beefed up with a 4-barrel carb to generate 380 horsepower. Another version of the 409 included three 2-barrel carbs for 409 horsepower. Race drivers Don Nicholson and Ronnie Sox would capture a number of Stock Eliminator titles that year while Hayden Proffit, in a '62 Bel Air bubbletop, clocked in at 12.83 seconds in the quarter-mile run, hitting a top speed of 113.63 mph (182.83kph) at the U.S. Nationals in Indianapolis.

GM's racing ban hurt Chevy's performance since no more factory lightweights were produced. Ford, when it later returned to racing, and Mopar achieved top-dog status for several years until Chevy returned to the game in the early 1970s with its 460-horsepower Chevelle.

In the early 1960s, Ford tried using fiberglass to shave some weight off its Galaxies. The '63 427-ci/425-hp high-performance Galaxie was equipped with a fiberglass hood, fenders, inner fenders, doors, and trunks. The front and rear bumpers were aluminum. Still, the Galaxie was one of the heavier lightweights at 3,500 pounds (1,590kg) (compared to the 3,360-pound [1,525kg] Chevy Bel Air, the 3,325-pound [1,510kg] Pontiac Catalina, the 3,300-pound [1,500kg] Dodge Ramcharger, the 3,350-pound [1,520kg] Plymouth Savoy, and the 2,600-pound [1,180kg] Mercury Comet). The Galaxie couldn't break the 12-second barrier, but could hit 120 mph (192kph).

The Ford Fairlane Thunderbolt models, of which 127 were built to qualify as production models to compete in Super Stock races, weighed considerably less than the Galaxie at 3,200 pounds (1,450kg). Powered by a 427-ci/425-hp engine with aluminum bumpers and fiberglass body parts, the Thunderbolt did exceptionally well, winning the NHRA Winternationals one year with an 11.78 time in the quarter mile and an overall speed of 123.4 mph (198.6kph).

The Comet, the little brother to the Galaxie and Fairlane, also fared well on the drag strip. Mercury in 1964 built a fleet of fifty lightweight Comets for the Factory Experimental drag racing events. The Comet was powered by a 427-ci/425-hp big block and did its best time ever at 10.56 seconds in a quarter mile. No wonder Mercury sold these limited production cars as "not for use on public highways."

OPPOSITE: *Interior of a stock Boss Ford Mustang. Factory lightweights offered the kind of power that once could only be achieved through careful tuning.*

CHRYSLER CUTS LOOSE IN THE 1990S

While nearly every Detroit automaker had its hand in developing factory hot rods, the Chrysler Corporation in recent years has taken the romance of the factory hot rod a step further. Today, Chrysler is perhaps the most bold in developing concept cars that evoke the heady days of factory-built muscle-bound cars. Chrysler, always ahead of the pack in engineering, debuted its Hemi-powered 300 letter-series models in the '50s and continued the tradition with the likes of the Dodge Charger and Challenger, the Plymouth Barracuda, and the Road Runner in the late '60s and early '70s.

Even the oil crisis and federal regulations didn't completely dim attempts by Chrysler to put more muscle under the hood. Between 1986 and 1989, Chrysler chairman Lee Iacocca recruited Carroll Shelby as a hired gun to produce limited editions of high-performance Dodges, including the Charger GTLH-S, the Shelby Lancer, the Shelby Dakota, and the turbocharged Shadow CSX-VNT.

Thus it's no surprise that the automaker continued to indulge in its attempts to achieve maximum satisfaction in testosterone-based supercars. Chrysler's first effort since the days of Shelby was the Dodge Viper. Close on its wheels was the Plymouth Prowler. The Prowler is the first-ever factory-built hot rod that comes with a warranty, a dealer service network, and dealer financing.

The Dodge Viper was first introduced as a concept car in 1989. It gave a nod to the European styling of the 1950s, but is strictly all-American right down to its multicylinder powerplant.

THE VIPER SHOWS ITS FANGS

The foundation of the Dodge Viper was established by a hearty group of stylists and engineers who were given the freedom to develop a machine independent of Chrysler. Indeed, the Viper team acted as their own private company during the various developmental stages of the car's creation.

The Viper RT/10 open-air roadster was introduced in 1989 as a concept car. The concept was completely American, from its multicylinder power plant to its vaguely retro styling, which emerged not as an imitation of roadsters from yesteryear but as a legend in its own time.

Dodge brass recognized in the late 1980s that the motoring public was ready for a beefy monster of a sports car that would not only satisfy the urge to open a roadster full throttle but maintain as well a sense of styling that would remain contemporary for decades. A team of engineers and stylists were handpicked mainly for their fanatical devotion to high-performance cars. They were encouraged to exist independently inside the Chrysler Corporation by creating their own rules and developing their own supplier base. Mavericks were encouraged to apply.

The team sought to build an aluminum engine and marry it to a high-performance chassis that could handle the stresses of brutal, high-speed driving. By the end of 1990, a V-8–powered mule, a chassis prototype, was tested. A few months later a cast-iron V-10 was built and tested. In May 1990, the first aluminum V-10 was on the test track. At the 1991 Indianapolis

500, the Viper RT/10 made its first practical debut as the official pace car. By January 1992, the first Vipers were ready for delivery to local dealers.

Each Viper is hand-assembled at Chrysler's 345,000-square-foot (32,085sqm) Conner Avenue plant in Detroit. Each chassis has its wheels aligned off its wheel hubs to improve the ride and handling. And each rolling chassis is tested up to 87 mph (139kph) at a computerized testing station to monitor the functions of the engine, transmission, and brakes under driving conditions.

The first Viper, the RT/10 roadster, is equipped with either the standard soft top that can be folded and stored in the trunk or the optional body-colored removable hard top that clamps into place. With a base price of $72,396, the roadster, like other Viper models, is placed on a 96.2-inch (244.3cm) wheelbase with an overall length of 175.1 inches (444.8cm). The V-10 aluminum block engine has a bore and stroke of 4 x 3.88 inches (10.2 x 9.9cm) and a 488-cubic-inch displacement. With a compression ratio of 9.6:1, it offers 450 braking horsepower at 5200 rpm and torque at 490 pounds-feet at 3700 rpm. The forged aluminum wheels are 10 x 17 inches (25 x 43cm) in the front and 13 x 17 inches (33 x 43cm) in the rear. The RT/10 tested at 4 seconds in 0–60 mph with a 12.2-second clocking in the quarter mile, with a top speed of 177 mph (283kph).

In *Motor Trend* road tests, the Dodge Viper GTS coupe, which is virtually identical to the roadster, handily beat the top foreign and domestic sports cars. The GTS, according to *Motor Trend*, hit a top speed of 193.2 mph (310.9kph) while the Porsche 911 Turbo hit 181.8 mph (292.5kph) and the Ferrari F353 achieved 180 mph (289.6kph). Only the Porsche 911 Turbo fared better than the Viper in 0–60 mph acceleration, at 3.7 seconds compared to the GTS's 4 seconds.

The racing version of the GTS, the GTS-R, captured first placed in the Overall Series of the 1997 GT-2 Manufacturers' World Championship. Powered by a 514-cubic-inch aluminum V-10 engine with a compression ratio of 10:1 and bore and stroke of 4.01 x 4.08 inches (10.2 x 10.4cm), the GTS-R generated 650 braking horsepower at 6000 rpm and 650 pounds-feet of torque at 5000 rpm. It could hit a top speed of 203 mph (325kph). But watch out. Base price for this puppy is $250,000.

The Viper also captured a pair of GT2 class wins in the FIA GT Series. To celebrate its victories, Dodge produced a limited edition of one hundred ultra-performance GT2 Championship Edition Vipers, painted in basic white and set off by broad blue racing stripes. The package includes a distinctive front splitter and a rear wing. Special badging and graphics include "Viper GTS-R" on the windshield and hood. The car is mounted on oversized Michelin tires on special 18-inch (46cm) BBS alloy wheels. The interior is covered in black leather and the driver and passenger are protected by special five-point seatbelts. Each car carries a serialized dash plaque. But the buyer pays for all these goodies. The price tag is $85,200.

While the Dodge Viper is hardly an "everyman" car, the Chrysler Corporation has continued to maintain its edge in developing the concept and building the high-performance machines that can kick butt on the track but also be available for the public road.

OPPOSITE: *Designers of the Dodge Viper were fanatical in their affection for sports cars, with the Chrysler Corp. urging maverick designers and engineers to apply to join the Dodge Viper team.*

PAGES **100–101:** *The V-10 aluminum block Dodge Viper engine has a 488-cubic-inch displacement and offers 450 braking horsepower at 5200 rpm. Its torque is rated at 490 pounds-feet at 3700 rpm.*

THE PROWLER TAKES OFF

The Prowler was the result of a brainstorming session in 1990 by staff members at Chrysler's Pacifica Design, a small studio just north of San Diego. The idea was to come up not only with good ideas but some outrageous ones as well. Nothing was too far out for possible designs. It's also no coincidence that as the 1990s dawned, the hot rod was making a comeback as baby boomers, achieving a comfortable income level, could afford to spend money on building their dream cars.

Whether Chrysler seized on this to produce the Prowler is up for debate. Still, the design folks did decide that a "retro car" reminiscent of the early highboy hot rod would startle the bejesus not only out of the motoring public but their Detroit competitors. "Retro," in some respects, has become a dirty word in marketing circles: capitalizing on nostalgia with a product that may have a shelf life of, say, two years only brings in quick bucks and is soon forgotten. But Chrysler stylists and engineers—determined to use huge amounts of aluminum for a lightweight frame and body and applying modern styles, surfaces, and other materials—developed a car that may have started as retro, but has emerged as a full-blown hot rod that is likely to endure into the twenty-first century.

Once Chrysler stylists got the green light to proceed with the project, they began popping up at local hot rod shows to get a feel for the subculture, and talked to as many hot rodders as they could before returning to the design table to take a crack at the specifics. Inspired by what they learned, the design team remained true to the art form of the hot rod. They rejected an early idea to use a retractable glass canopy

The Plymouth division at Chrysler deliberately went for the retro look by copying the famed highboys of the 1930s. Motorcycle fenders and eyebrow front bumpers don't detract from the graceful lines of this highly unusual factory hot rod.

by agreeing that a fabric convertible top better emulated the spirit of the hot rod. They also decided early on that purple reflected the Prowler's personality, although a brilliant yellow—an homage to a favorite hot rod color—would appear on 1999 models.

Putting an emphasis on aluminum construction, the Prowler is 21 percent lighter than it would be were it made of conventional components. The body, frame, and suspension system are constructed of aluminum, and account for 900 pounds (410kg) of the car's total weight of 2,838 pounds (1,289kg). That's pretty good considering that the Prowler is a "parts-bin" car that uses mechanical parts from the Viper, Neon, Jeep Cherokee, Dodge Caravan, Cirrus, and assorted Dodge trucks.

To complement the Prowler's needle-nose and hefty rear end with a more a rakish look, 17 x 7.5-inch (43 x 19cm) cast aluminum wheels were placed on the front, with 20 x 10-inch (51 x 25cm) wheels on the rear. The wheelbase measures 113.3 inches (287.8cm) with an overall length of 165.3 inches (419.9cm). The front bumper was a special problem: true hot rods did without them, but modern federal impact standards demand protection. Designers settled on a split bumper that appears to be floating just ahead of the car's cycle fenders. While the front bumper has generated some controversy for its awkward appearance, it actually works reasonably well with the coil springs mounted inboard, much like a modern formula single-seat race car. With the springs out of sight and out of the air stream, the bumpers give fairly clean lines.

The dashboard gauges are pure retro, with the 150-mph (240kph) speedometer, odometer, and fuel, ammeter, oil, and temperature gauges in a clean, straight line. The 7000 rpm tach is mounted on the steering column, to make any rodder's heart flutter with adolescent nostalgia for their high school street-racing days. A 6-cylinder engine under the hood of such a hot rod forty years ago would have been laughed off the hamburger stand parking lot or run off the boulevard. But it makes sense in the Prowler.

It's powered by a V-6 3518-cc 24-valve fuel-injected engine with a compression ratio of 10.1:1 to generate 253 braking horsepower at 6400 rpm and 255 pounds-feet of torque at 3950 rpm. It would have been a nice touch to have a manual transmission installed, but the Prowler sports a four-speed electronically controlled AutoStick automatic transmission. The tranny, however, is state of the art, with a rear-wheel transaxle that is similar to that of the high-tech Porsche 928S and 968. Stopping power comes from four-wheel disc brakes. The price tag for this baby runs about $38,000, which ain't bad considering that the Dodge Viper commands a price of around $70,000.

OPPOSITE: *Yellow was the new color for 1999 Plymouth Prowlers.*

BELOW: *This isn't the interior of your grandfather's Ford deuce coupe, but a no-nonsense, high-tech '90s approach to styling and comfort. Note the tachometer attached to the steering column.*

CHAPTER 5

PICK *UPS*

Pickup trucks, long the workhorses of farmers and urban haulers, are finally gaining some overdue respect. Once scoffed at by hot rodders as well as the urban elite, pickups are becoming the most popular vehicles on city streets as well as country roads. They have become today's ponycars: inexpensive, powerful, and customizable. In the last twenty years the customization of the pickup truck has steadily gained momentum.

In recent years, the NASCAR Craftsman Truck Series, which began in 1995, has heightened the awareness of trucks as the hot rods of today. With NASCAR's endorsement, the pickup truck today has become what the deuce coupe was fifty years ago—the new and exciting street brute. And the public is tapping into the new hobby: since 1971, annual truck sales have climbed from 2,096,126 to 6,481,357, while passenger car sales have dropped from 10,242,205 to 8,634,998, according to the American Automobile Manufacturers Association. Pickup trucks are hot, and it's not uncommon for them to be hot rods.

The Ford F-150 continues to be the top dog in annual truck sales, while the full-size Chevrolet C/K pickup saw its sales in 1996 climb 29 percent over the previous year's figures. And Chrysler, thanks in large part to the dramatically restyled full-size Dodge Ram and medium-size Dakota pickups, saw sales rise 7 percent in 1996 over 1995 sales.

The demographics for full-size pickup truck owners have changed significantly since the days when trucks were used solely for hauling goods and materials. Today's average pickup truck owner has a median income of more than $50,000; 50 percent of pickup owners have attended college, and more than 40 percent of them are employed in professional or managerial capacities. Nearly 40 percent of pickup owners are under forty-five years old. It's no coincidence that these numbers also reflect in varying degrees the hot rod owner.

ONE SOUPED-UP PICKUP

Butch Lee's Pro-Mod pickup hits the apex of what a customized hot rod should be. His '95 Chevrolet Sportside was the first pickup to break the 7-second barrier in the quarter-mile run when it hit 6.79 seconds. Owner of Main Street Auto in Mesa, Arizona, Lee performed most of the work on his Chevy himself. Under the fiberglass clip is a massive 526-cubic-inch Rodeck engine with a 12:1 compression ratio that develops a whopping 2,000 horsepower. Lee selected the cream of the crop from the parts bin by installing a Crane cam, Cola crankshaft, Clevite bearings, Venolia pistons, Jessel rockers, Brooks rods, Indy heads, and Enderle fuel injection. A Super Mag IV

PAGE 106: *This '92 Chevrolet pickup is virtually stock on the outside, but heavy in factory options with the hood scoop, front spoiler, and bed cover.*

PAGE 107: *Custom hubcaps are the first step toward a hot rod pickup.*

RIGHT: *Another Chevrolet pickup truck, this one a Silverado that is heavily optioned from the factory. Note the front bumper treatment, special chrome wheels, and side exhausts.*

ignition system, titanium valves, and an Optima battery also were installed. Power is transferred through a Lenco three-speed transmission. At the rear is a 4.56-geared Mark Williams Ford 9-inch.

Lee built a roll cage attached to a chrome chassis. Inside is a racer's no-nonsense dream: custom seats equipped with Deist harnesses, a Mark Williams steering wheel, and Auto Meter gauges. The sheet-metal work, paint, and graphics were farmed out to Squeeg's Kustom in Mesa.

Lee's Chevy is a lesson in extreme customizing and a pickup not likely to be cruising the local boulevards. Rather, the Ford F-100 has laid claim to being perhaps the pickup truck of choice to customize, chop, and channel as local street fare. Brad Romaine of Julian, California, has a '56 Ford F-100 that is powered by a '68 Ford 351-ci/302-hp engine with an Edelbrock carb. Its power is transferred with a Ford C4 tranny and B&M

shift kit. Much of its chassis and suspension components came from a NASCAR Winston Cup Thunderbird and the "9 Car" that captured the 1988 Pepsi Firecracker 400 at Daytona.

The '68 Chevrolet pickup also serves well as a Pro Street truck. Richard Kohler of DeSoto, Missouri, had his Chevy's roof chopped 3 inches (7.5cm) for a lower look, then installed a 454 to make as much power as possible. The 454 features stock heads and valve covers but is fed through a 750 cfm Holley carb. To give it an extra oomph, a set of Hooker headers and Turbo mufflers were installed. The power from the 454 is transferred through a TH400 tranny and B&M 3000 stall speed converter to a '70 Chrysler 8 3/4-inch (22cm) rear end with a 4.56:1 gear ratio. Kohler customized it a bit by carving "Bow Tie" turn signals into the front bumpers, then having it painted DuPont Cromo 1 black, complemented with a gray tweed interior.

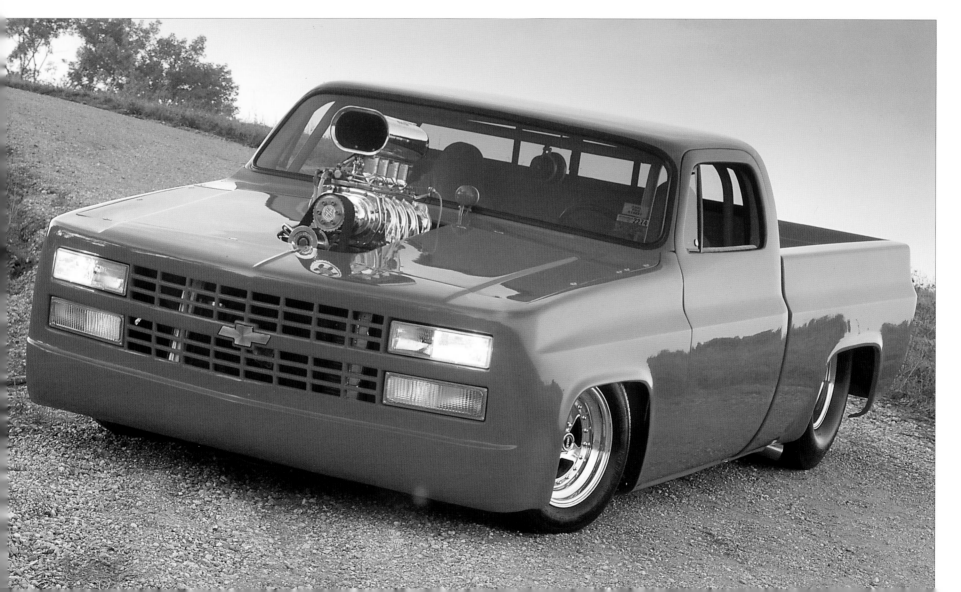

A CLASSIC PICKUP:
THE FORD F-100 SERIES

Why would a pickup more than four decades old entice an owner to invest in state-of-the-art components? Much of the answer lies in the timeless beauty and elegance of the classic Ford F-100 truck line. Studebaker caught the light-truck industry by surprise in 1949, when it introduced its sleek R-Series pickups, but Ford carried that stylishness a step further with the F-100 series trucks, which debuted in 1953.

The Ford Motor Company wanted to celebrate its fiftieth anniversary in 1953 with a bang. Its 1948–52 "Bonus Built" trucks served their purpose as Ford's first postwar design for its light-duty truck line, but by the early '50s the design had become stodgy and out of date. Ford was so determined to come up with the best-looking pickup that it invested $50 million in research. For the 1953 model year, Ford designers and engineers came up with a tall cab, smartly angled curved windshield, and a simple, but heavy, horizontal chrome grille. The curved windshield and 4-foot-wide (1.2m) rear window

improved visibility. The 56.7-inch-wide (144cm) bench seat allowed enough room for three people. In addition to the improved cab, the 6-1/2-foot (2m) box was decorated with seasoned wood protected by steel strips.

Ford's investment resulted in sales of 116,437 trucks for 1953. It's one of the few trucks that has endured generation after generation as the truck of choice. It was a truck that captured the imagination of the buying public—and the perfect truck for hot rodding. The F-Series continues today as the F-150 Series.

BEYOND THE F-100

While the Ford F-100 remains one of the most popular trucks to customize, panel trucks too have gained attention in hot rodding circles. Powered by the venerable flathead V-8 and once used almost exclusively for deliveries and ambulance duty, the panel truck has found a renewed life as a street and custom rod.

Dennis Overholser of Texas owns a '36 Ford panel truck that performed laundry-delivery duty in the 1930s and '40s. Taking to what amounted to a mess, Overholser sandblasted, painted, and polished all parts and powder-coated the frame before reassembly. The front suspension was lifted from a Mustang II and the rear springs came off a Plymouth Volare. The shocks at the four corners are Pro Shocks and the power

steering rack was hooked to the Ididit chrome steering column with Borgeson steering components.

Under the hood is a Ford SVO 5-liter fuel-injected engine powered with a C6 B&M transmission. The interior includes Rod Doors door panels with the seats and padding done in Platinum Ultra Leather by Leon Brown Upholstery in Texas. The dashboard sports Auto M Street Rod gauges. Also decked out inside is a Grant Banjo steering wheel, Downs Manufacturing power windows, and a Sherwood stereo system.

Factory-customized trucks, especially the recent additions of the Dodge Ram and Dakota, as well as elaborate aftermarket packages for virtually any new pickup truck on the road, have boosted interest among collectors seeking to create highly individualized custom and street rods in old or even late model trucks.

OPPOSITE: *The Shelby team has even taken a swipe at the growing SUV market; this Ford Explorer is all decked out in Shelby's trademark racing stripes.*

RIGHT: *This is a rare custom specimen: a 1998 Dodge Durango sport utility vehicle. Heavily customized from the ground up with factory options, this SUV sports a damper, triple headlamps, custom wheels and much more.*

BELOW: *A Dodge Ram pickup receives rear spoiler treatment in addition to a damper and custom grille.*

PAGE 116–117: *The '34 Ford Woodie remains a popular choice for the car and truck enthusiast. The owner of this hot rod remained true to its original factory design, but subtle touches to the wheels and paint scheme make it a standout among any truck or station wagon competition.*

BIBLIOGRAPHY

Barris, George, and David Fetherston. *Barris Kustoms of the 1950s*. Osceola, Wisconsin: Motorbooks International, 1994.

Brown, Arch. "1968–72 Buick GS & GSX: Gentleman's Muscle Car." *Collectible Automobile*, June 1994.

Dammann, George H. *75 Years of Chevrolet*. Sarasota, Florida: Crestline Publishing, 1986.

Flammang, James M. *Standard Catalog of Imported Cars, 1946–1990*. Iola, Wisconsin: Krause Publications, 1994.

General Motors Public Relations Department/Chevrolet. *50 Years of the Hot Rod*: (Limited special collector's edition). Np: Petersen Publishing Co., 1998.

Gunnell, John, editor. *Standard Catalog of American Cars, 1946–1975*. Iola, Wisconsin: Krause Publications, 1992.

Hossain, Tony. "1968–72 Chevrolet Chevelle: The Sleek and Sporty Second Generation." *Collectible Automobile*, October 1994.

Patino, Marco A. "Evil Ways." *Lowrider* Magazine Online (www.lowridermagazine.com).

Penland, Paige R. "Grapenutz." *Lowrider* Magazine Online.

Penland, Paige R. "Lowrider Magazine History." *Lowrider* Magazine Online.

Penland, Paige R. "Malo '63." *Lowrider* Magazine Online.

Rick, Jeffrey. "Aztlan Nation." *Lowrider* Magazine Online.

Unknown author. "Street Tattoo II." *Lowrider* Magazine Online.

Van Kirk, B.T. "1961–64 Chevrolet Impala/SS: Ride, Room and Zoom." *Collectible Automobile*, December 1989.

Vargas, Saul. "It's Time for Bubblicious." *Lowrider* Magazine Online.

Weesner, Jerry. "Sniper." *Custom Rodder*, July 1998.

Woods, Bill. "New From Mother." *Mopar Action*, June 1997.

PHOTO CREDITS

Photography by Randy Lorentzen

© Walt Weis: 63 both

INDEX